John Almon

A letter concerning libels, warrants, the seizure of papers and sureties for the peace or behaviour

With a view to some late proceedings. Third Edition

John Almon

A letter concerning libels, warrants, the seizure of papers and sureties for the peace or behaviour
With a view to some late proceedings. Third Edition

ISBN/EAN: 9783337225087

Printed in Europe, USA, Canada, Australia, Japan

Cover: Foto ©Andreas Hilbeck / pixelio.de

More available books at **www.hansebooks.com**

A LETTER

CONCERNING

LIBELS, WARRANTS,

THE

SEIZURE of PAPERS,

AND

SURETIES for the PEACE or BEHAVIOUR;

WITH A

VIEW to some late PROCEEDINGS,

AND THE

DEFENCE of Them by the MAJORITY.

The THIRD EDITION,
ENLARGED and IMPROVED.

The Child may rue, that is unborn,
The Hunting of that Day. CHEVY CHASE.

LONDON:
Printed for J. ALMON, opposite *Burlington House* in *Piccadilly*. 1765.

A LETTTR

TO

Mr. ALMON,

BEING AN

ENQUIRY, &c.

SIR,

SOME weeks after my son's sending you *A Letter to the Public Advertiser*, I was surprized with the sight of a * pamphlet, wherein a contrary doctrine is conveyed, altho' I cannot say directly affirmed; from which last circumstance I guess it to be the work of some enterprizing Attorney, retouched by his Superior.

The Attorney begins by reproaching others with " wretched quibbling upon words, misrepresentation, igno- " rance, blundering and falshoods," and then represents himself and his friends as " reasoning men, of knowledge, " integrity and ability;" but I suspect nevertheless, from the sophistry one now and then meets with in his argumentation, that he has had the assistance of another man " who has been taught to think himself a Statesman, and who would be too happy to be able to think himself a minister," and to whom I shall only say, as he loves a classic,

Vane *Ligur*, frustraque animis elate superbis,
Nequicquam *patrias* tentasti *lubricus* artes.

I shall not dispute the knowledge or ability either of the one as a dexterous Common-lawyer, or of the other as a versatile Logician; and as to public integrity, they need so little be questioned, that it would be now-a-days the idlest

* The Majority defended.

of pastimes in any man to urge a syllable upon that head concerning either; altho' I remember that one of them, during the last rebellion, would never in his public speeches venture to call the rebel army any other than the *Highland Army*, for fear, I presume, of spoiling his fortune, in case it succeeded. The Attorney, however, has ventured to assert in print, what I do not remember to have heard any one gentleman avow in parliament, and for that reason, among others, has attracted my notice and indignation.

Indeed, the discourse of late has run so much upon libels, warrants, and resolutions of parliament, that every body's thoughts have been turned to these points. Now, I do not think myself at liberty to scan the private actions of any man, but have a right to consider the conduct of every man in public; and to approve or to condemn his doings as they appear to me to be calculated, either for the good or the hurt of his country.

A King of England may be considered in two respects, either in a public or private capacity. In the latter he may, as a man, indulge his own humour, in the establishment of his houshold and the choice of his immediate servants. But in the former, he is wholly a creature of polity; his crown, his power, and his revenue are derived from and circumscribed by act of parliament. He is indeed the first in rank of the three independent parts of the legislature, and the executive hand of the whole; but the ministers and officers by which he carries on the government are the servants of the community, and the public weal is the sole object of the intire political frame. In order, however, to preserve a proper respect and chastity of idea with regard to the crowned head, the royal name is never to be introduced into any question of public transactions. And therefore it is established as a maxim *The King can do no wrong*; as doing nothing of himself, but every thing by the advice of his council and ministers. The speeches from the throne; treaties of peace and war; the application of public revenue; appointments to offices in the state; the direction of crown-prosecutions; and, in a word, every other act of government must be always debated, questioned, and blamed as the acts of the minister. As nothing can be done in a limited monarchy, but what somebody is to be accountable for it, so every

minister

minister in his department is to be responsible accordingly, and to act at his peril.

There is no inseparable connection between a minister and the Sovereign. The latter is not, by the duty of his office, to support any one man against the general sentiments of his people; and of course, whatever is said, or written against the administration, is not to be regarded as an attack upon his throne. Indeed, were it otherwise, no act of a minister could ever be arraigned, and no liberty of the press exist; for, every inquiry, and censure in print, would be sowing sedition, if not high treason, in the state.

By the old constitution, and afterwards by Magna Charta, no man could be put upon his trial for any offence, until a grand Jury had found a bill of indictment, or, of their own knowledge, made a presentment thereof. By degrees however, and by virtue of particular statutes, crimes against the peace became presentable by conservators or justices of the peace. In process of time, misdemeanors came to be prosecuted by an information filed by the King's coroner or Attorney, that is, the master of the crown office; and this was considered as the presentment of the King. A petty jury was afterwards to try the truth of every such indictment, presentment or information. But, Henry the 7th, one of the worst Princes this nation ever knew, procured an act of parliament which, after reciting many defects and abuses in trials by jury, and pretending a remedy for the same, gives a summary jurisdiction to certain great officers of state, calling to them a bishop, to summon, try and punish, of their own mere discretion and authority, any persons who shall be accused of the offences therein very generally named and described. In short, the court of starchamber is, by this act, so enlarged in its jurisdiction, that it may be said to be erected, and both grand and petit juries in crown matters are in great measure laid aside, as the Attorney-general now brings every thing of that sort before this court, which, by its constitution, never can make use of either. In lieu of an indictment or presentment of their peers, people of all degrees are put on their trial by a charge framed at the pleasure of the Attorney-general, called an information, and filed by him without even the sanction of an oath; and the star chamber decide thereon most

B 2 con-

conscientiously, but, as most true courtiers would wish to do, without the intervention of a jury. The faces of the subject are so ground by this proceeding, that every body at length is alarmed, and the people in struggling with the crown happening to get the better, the patriots of the time seized an occasion, towards the latter end of the reign of Charles the First, to extort from that martyr to obstinacy, an act for the abolition of this most oppressive jurisdiction. But, by some fatality, the Attorney-general's information, was overlooked and suffered still to remain, and the use that is now made of it every body knows. It is reported, however, that my Lord Chief Justice Hale had so little opinion of the legality of this kind of informations, that he used to say, "If ever they came in dispute, they " could not stand, but must necessarily fall to the ground."

It was also long thought, they could only be filed where the King was immediately concerned; and so the old books say; but, it is now certain that they are not limited by any thing besides the discretion of the Attorney-general, who is an officer of the Crown, *durante bene placito*, and not upon oath. They may, in time, become an ordinary engine of Administration, as much as any Gazette or common Courier. Indeed, the secresy, ease and certainty of laying a man under a heavy prosecution in the Crown-office, without any controul, by this mode of information, are what render it much more formidable than the common, regular information, which can now only be filed by virtue of a statute passed soon after the revolution, upon the Prosecutor entring into a recognizance and by leave of the King's Bench, after a public hearing in open court. Indeed, there is this very dreadful circumstance attending, the Crown never pays any costs; so that it can harrass the peace of any man in the realm, and put him to a grievous expence, without ever trying the matter at all. Indeed, the costs of the Crown-office are so enormous, that any man of middling circumstances, will be undone by two or three plunges there. Most Booksellers and Printers know this very well, and hence so few of them can be got to publish a stricture upon any administration.

It is a power that is, in my apprehension, very alarming; and a thinking man cannot refrain from surprize, that a free people should suffer so odious a prerogative

tive to exist. It has been, and may most certainly be again, the means of great persecution. In truth, it seems to be a power necessary for no good purpose, and capable of being put to a very bad one. For, although a man may doubt whether a Grand Jury in times of violent party, would always find a bill of indictment or present, yet there can be none but that a Court of *King's Bench* would grant an information, wherever it could, by any Administration, be applied for with the least foundation. It is still more wonderful that, since this prerogative is endured, there has been no act passed to subject the Attorney-General, provided he did not pursue his information, or upon trial was nonsuited, or had a verdict against him, to the payment of full costs to the party abused.

This very game was played with a late Vice-Chancellor of Oxford, when L. H. was of the Cabinet, and at the head of the law. The Attorney General filed an information *ex officio*, and, after putting the Doctor to a vast expence, entered a *nolle prosequi*. Soon after he filed another information for the same offence, and, when a like expence was incurred, entered another *nolle prosequi*. In short, this politico-legal game was had resort to, because there was no evidence to convict, and was dropped and renewed in order to oppress, to the extreme charge of the worthless Doctor, and to the infinite discredit of a moderate King. During the reign of this Law-Lord, the same Star-chamber weapon was frequently brandished, like *Medusa's* head, to terrify and benum individuals. A secret and efficacious method of preserving the peace! Many an useful publication has been nipped in the bud by an information *ex officio* (that great suppressor of truth) and by the gripe of its executioner, (that enemy to light) the messenger of the press. An information has been frequently filed, and the miserable object of it awed into giving security for his future behaviour, without any legal ground for either, or serious design of prosecution; and in this ignominious state of apprehension and bondage has he been kept for years together, without either being ever withdrawn.

The oppression, however, can go no farther; for, if that trial proceeds, the security of Englishmens rights, a Jury must be called in. Some late statutes, however, (I

should

should just observe) in particular instances have given a summary and final jurisdiction to Justices of the Peace, in matters of Excise, Game, &c. where the proceedings and decisions are arbitrary, vexatious and partial enough I believe; but this does not reach to such a length as to endanger, perhaps, the Constitution itself.

There is no offence which is oftener prosecuted by an information, *ex officio*, than a libel. Now, many Judges before the Revolution, and perchance some since, have said that, in law, a paper may be a libel, whether the charges in it be true or false, against a good or a bad man, the living or the dead; nay, that the truth of it is even an aggravation of the crime: that every libel is, by construction of law, even against the peace, and (in very late times) that it is an actual breach of the peace; and (at last) that securities for the good behaviour may be demanded of any man, charged with being the Author, Printer or Publisher. After all, I do not yet learn by what certain signs one can know whether any particular pamphlet or paper will induce any body to commit a breach of the peace.

I think one may say of the Lawyers, who have thus matured the doctrine of informations, that they have been very astute in the forging of chains for mankind. Nothing, indeed, can be added but the revival of a position, to be met with likewise in some few cases before the Revolution, that a Jury is only to try the fact of publication, and must leave the intention of the words to the Court, for their construction; unless, indeed, it could be contrived to get rid of Juries intirely, that is, to establish in perfection the Star-Chamber anew. Already, almost any thing that a man writes may, by the help of that useful and ingenious key to construction, an inuendo, be explained to scandalize Government, and of course be a libel; and could the last mentioned impediments be totally removed, instead of being only now and then got the better of by the dexterity of a Judge, no writing whatever could possibly escape conviction.

However, it is only in conformity with common parlance, that I speak of law and fact in libel as distinct things; to myself they appear to be inseparably united. For, a criminal prosecution and trial can only be had for a crime; now the mere simple publication of any thing not libellous

(there

(there being no public licenser) is no crime at all; it is then the publication of what is false, scandalous and seditious, that is the crime, and solely gives jurisdiction to the criminal Court; and That therefore is what must, of necessity, be submitted to the Jury for their opinion and determination. A decisive argument to the same purpose may be drawn from the conduct of the Lawyers themselves in this very matter. For, it is agreed, on all hands, to be necessary for the Crown-Pleader to set forth specially some passages of the paper, and to charge it to be a false, or malicious libel. Now, this would never be done by the Law-Pleaders, submitted to by the Attorney-General, or endured by the Judges, if it was not essential to the legality of the proceeding. The King's Bench, in granting the information, only act like a Grand Jury in finding a bill of indictment, and in effect say no more than this, That, so far as appears to them, the paper charged seems to be a libel, and therefore the person accused should be put upon his trial before a Jury, whose business it will be to enter thoroughly into the matter, hear the evidence examined, and what the Council can say on both sides, and form a judgment upon the whole, which, after such a discussion, it will not be difficult for any men of common understanding to do. Whether the contents of the paper be true, or false, or malicious, is a fact to be collected from circumstances, as much as whether a trespass be wilful or not, or the killing of a man with malice forethought. "Whether any act was done or any word "spoken, in such or such a manner, or with such or such "an intent, the Jurors are Judges. The Court is not "Judge of these matters which are evidence to prove or "disprove the thing in issue." This is our law, both in civil and criminal trials, altho' the latter are by far the most material, because what affects our person, liberty or life is of more consequence than what merely affects our property.

Were I therefore a Juror, I should take nothing implicitly or upon trust, in this respect, from any man, but should endeavour to form my own judgment of the matter as an impartial Juror, and not as a Statesman: plain truth and fact, and common sense, and not political convenience, far-fetched inference, or ingenious inuendo, being the proper object and intent of my oath by the law
of

of the land. "The verdict itself is not an act ministerial, but judicial, and where the Jurors give it according to the best of their judgment, they are not finable. They can only be punished by attaint, that is, by another Jury, where it shall be found that wilfully they gave a verdict false and corrupt. Indeed, were this not so, they would be but mere ecchos to sound back the pleasure of the court." Whereas Judges cannot refuse to receive a Jury's verdict.

The strict law I know, is pretended to be, that the truth of the matter asserted is no defence against the charge of its being a libel; but that is a point which I shall never be prevailed upon to receive as law, from the authority of any man whatever; and much the less so, for the fashion now introducing (for the first time since the Revolution) of proceeding against Printers after the Author is known, which breaths a spirit of persecution (I may say of cruelty) hardly to be endured.

The statutes against Slander and Scandalum magnatum, (namely the 3d Ed. I. 2d and 12th Ric. II.) direct only that he who "shall be so hardy to tell or publish any false news or tales, whereby discord or slander may grow between the King and his people, or the great men of the realm, shall be taken and kept in prison until he has brought *him* into the Court *which was the first Author of the tale.*"

If an Attorney-General finds it necessary in law to charge a paper to be false, in order to render his information against it, as a libel, legal; and that his informing against it for being a *true* libel, would not only be ridiculous, but bad in law, he should prove it to be false, or I would never upon my oath find it to be so, let what measure or what magistrate soever be the object of it; in reality, it would be absurd to do otherwise. Indeed, the distinction between words spoken and words written is most curious. For no criminal prosecution lies for words spoken, and none are even actionable in themselves that do not impute a crime; their truth may be pleaded in justification, no inuendo is permitted, a Jury assesses the damages, and no greater costs than damages can be recovered. The calling of names and using of abusive language, is not actionable at all, and to ground an action some special damage must be alledged and proved. Otherways you can only proceed in the Court-Christian for an ecclesiastical censure. But, if the same words are committed to paper, the writer is a libeller, may be indicted or informed against, is admitted to plead nothing in his justification, and, if found guilty, may be fined and corporally punished, as the *King's-Bench* Judges shall think fit.

In truth, the Crown, in libel, should not only prove the words to be false, but likewise shew, either from the nature of the paper itself, or from external proof, that it was malicious as well as false, or I would acquit the defendant. For, if this were not likewise requisite, it might very well happen, that a sober and temperate man, who wrote very justly upon the whole against a bad ministry, might have been misinformed, touching some particular fact; and then the Attorney-General, after admitting or not contesting twenty other charges, might lay his finger upon this single one, and shew it to be false, and thereupon insist upon having made good his information. In such case, I should consider whether it was maliciously or wantonly, that the author had published such an untruth, or whether common fame supported him in it, and should acquit or condemn him accordingly; for, common fame has been resolved to be a good ground of accusation.

In short, the whole of the information is given in charge to the Jury, and if they find him guilty at all, they must find him guilty of the whole, that is, that by publishing such paper he is guilty of a libel; and if they do find this, it is not in the power of the King's-Bench afterwards to determine that the same was no libel. Therefore the charge both of the falsehood and the malice of the paper accused, as well as the fact of publication, should be made appear, or the Author and Publisher should be acquitted. The very statutes against slandering great men only punish false news and tales, *horrible and false* lies.

Judge *Powell*, in the trial of the seven Bishops, speaking of their petition, which was charged as a libel, in the information, said, " To make it a libel, it must be false " and malicious, and tend to sedition;" and declared, " As he saw no falsehood or malice in it, that it was no " libel." The other three Judges, it is true, were of a different opinon; but their opinion has ever since been held infamous, and his in the utmost veneration. Indeed,

Sir *Robert Sawyer*, as Council, infifted, in the fame trial, that " the falfity, the malice, and *fedition* of the writing, " were *all* facts to be proved." And it is faid, that Lord Chief Juftice *Holt* always afked, " Can you prove this to " be true? If you write fuch things as you are charged " with, it lies upon you to prove them true, at your " peril;" and a man runs rifk enough in being forced to do this. Mr. *Hawles*, in his excellent Treatife upon the duty of Petty Juries, called *The Englifhman's Right*, fays, " When the matter in iffue, is of fuch a nature, as
" no action, indictment or information will lie for it
" fingly, but it is worked up by fpecial aggravations into
" matter of damage or crime, as, that it was done to
" *fcandalize the government, raife fedition, affront autho-*
" *rity*, or the like, or with fuch or fuch an evil intent :
" if thefe aggravations, or fome *overt* act to manifeft fuch
" ill defign be not made out in evidence, then ought the
" Jury to find the party *Not Guilty*. And if a Jury fhall
" refufe to find that fuch an act was done *falfly, fcanda-*
" *loufly, malicioufly*, with an intent to *raife fedition, de-*
" *fame the government*, or the like, their mouths are not
" to be ftopped, or their confciences fatisfied, with the
" Court's telling them *You have nothing to do with that*,
" *it's only matter of form or matter of law, you are only*
" *to examine the fact, whether he fpoke fuch words, writ*
" *or fold fuch a book, or the like :* for, if they fhould igno-
" rantly take this for an anfwer, and bring in the prifoner
" *Guilty*, tho' they mean of the *naked* fact only, yet
" the Clerk recording it demands a further confirmation
" thus, *Then you fay D. is guilty of the trefpafs or mifde-*
" *meanor in manner and form as he ftands indicted, and fo*
" *you fay all?* And the verdict is drawn up, *The Jurors*
" *do fay, upon their oaths, that D. malicioufly, in contempt*
" *of the King and the government, with an intent to fcan-*
" *dalize the Adminiftration of Juftice, and to bring the fame*
" *into contempt, or to raife fedition*, &c. (as the words
" were laid) *fpake fuch words, publifhed fuch a book, or did*
" *fuch an act, againft the Peace of our Lord the King, his*
" *crown and dignity*."

Befides, there is a conftitutional reafon of infinite moment to a free people, Why a Jury fhould of themfelves always determine whether any thing be or be not a libel. It is this, that ninety-nine times out of an hundred, thefe
in-

informations for public libels are a dispute between the ministers and the people; and, in my conscience, this very circumstance has made our Progenitors retain to themselves the power of determining both the law and the fact, with respect to libels, altho' they waved or ceded to the Judges the power of determining the law in all other respects. . Having acquiesced in the power exercised by the Attorney General, of informing against what he pleases as a libel, they were resolved not to part with the prerogative of judging finally upon the matter themselves; and, in my poor opinion, had they done so, we should, long before this, not only have lost the liberty of the press, but every other liberty besides. No man that disapproved the measures of a court, would venture to discuss the propriety or consequence of them. No man would venture to utter a syllable in print against any power of office, and much less against any royal prerogative, however illegally usurped. He would be sure to be charged with a libel by the Attorney General, and to be fined, and perhaps imprisoned without mercy, by the *King's-Bench*, as, in fact, happened to Sir Samuel Bernardiston, whose judgment was reversed by Parliament after the Revolution.

Before that glorious æra, the Judges held their places at the King's pleasure, and acted accordingly. Their oath was then their only restraint; that was some guard, but not a sufficient one, when the consequence of a non-compliance with Administration would deprive a Judge of his livelihood, and raise the indignation and resentment of the Crown. Judges are now for life, and a noble security it is; and yet, unless one could insure them from the common failings of mankind, from ambition, the desire of promoting their children, or, if they have no children, of providing for their nephews, one may easily conceive that some influence may still take place even in a Judge.

But it is become more necessary than ever, that the people should retain the privilege of determining the law and the fact, relative to libels, because their representatives have lately, by a resolution declared, that *privilege of parliament does not extend to the case of a libel.* I had been always in an error upon this head before, which I was led into by old cases. My notion was not taken up in consequence of the construction made by the present Court of Common Pleas, nor did I, indeed, entirely build upon my own

own sense of the matter; but I was fixed in the opinion by the authority of that great lawyer Lord Chancellor *Egerton*, who, after having held the great seal for fourteen years, with greater reputation than any man before him, in a solemn argument which he delivered in the case of the *Post-Nati*, and which he afterwards published himself, upon a strict review, and with great deliberation, (so that it is uncontrovertibly his opinion) has laid down the same doctrine, and cites particularly the old determination made by the Judges in the case of Thorpe. His Lordship there says, " Then let us see what the wisdom of parliaments
" in times past, attributed to the Judges opinions declar-
" ed in parliament, of which there may be many exam-
" ples. In the parliament anno 31 H. 6, in the vacation
" (the parliament being continued by prorogation) *Thomas*
" *Thorpe*, the Speaker, was condemned in a thousand
" pounds damages, in an action of trespass brought against
" him by the Duke of *York*, and was committed to prison
" in execution for the same. After, when the parliament
" was re-assembled, the Commons made suit to the King
" and the Lords, to have *Thorpe*, the Speaker, delivered,
" for the good exploit of the parliament; whereupon the
" Duke of York's counsel declared the whole case at
" large. The Lords demanded the opinion of the Judges,
" whether, in that case, *Thorpe* ought to be delivered
" out of prison by privilege of parliament: the Judges
" made this answer, That they ought not to determine
" the privilege of that High Court of Parliament; but,
" for the declaration of proceeding in lower Courts, in
" cases where writs of supersedeas for the privilege of the
" parliament be brought unto them, they answered,
" That if any person that is a Member of Parliament be
" arrested, in such cases as be not for treason or felony, or
" for *surety of peace*, or condemnation had before the
" parliament, it is used that such persons be released, and
" may make Attorney, so as they may have their freedom
" and liberty freely to attend the parliament."

The Lords, in the following reign, most solemnly ratified this doctrine, in the famous case of the Earl of *Arundel*, by a resolution *nemine contradicente*; and then presented to the King, the following remonstrance, " May
" it please your Majesty, we the Peers of this your realm,
" now assembled in parliament, finding the Earl of
Arundel

" *Arundel* absent from his place, that sometimes in this
" parliament sat amongst us, his presence was therefore
" called for; but, hereupon a message was delivered unto
" us from your Majesty by the Lord Keeper, that the Earl
" of *Arundel* was restrained for a *misdemeanor*, which was
" personal to your Majesty, and had no relation to matter
" of parliament: this message occasioned us to enquire
" into the acts of our ancestors, and what in like cases
" they had done, that so we might not err in any duti-
" ful respect to your Majesty, and yet preserve our right
" and privilege of parliament: and after diligent search
" both of all stories, statutes and records that might in-
" form us in this case, we find it to be an undoubted
" right and constant privilege, That no Lord of Parlia-
" ment, sitting in the parliament, or within the usual times
" of privilege of parliament, is to be imprisoned or re-
" strained (without sentence or order of the house) unless
" it be for treason or felony, or *for refusing to give secu-
" rity for the peace*; and to satisfy ourselves the better,
" we have heard all that could be alleged by your Ma-
" jesty's learned Council at Law, that might any way in-
" fringe or weaken this claim of the Peers, and to all that
" claim be shewed and alledged, so full satisfaction has
" been given us that all the Peers in parliament, upon the
" question made of this privilege, have *una voce* consented
" that this is the undoubted right of the Peers, and inviol-
" ably has been enjoyed by them."

Now what my reasoning from such premises must be, may be easily guessed. It was thus: Members are clearly intitled to Privilege in all misdemeanors, for which sureties of the peace cannot be demanded. But, sureties of the peace cannot be demanded but in actual breaches of the peace. The writing of any thing quietly in one's study, and publishing it by the press, can certainly be no actual breach of the peace. Therefore, a Member who is only charged with this, cannot thereby forfeit his Privilege.

I thought that no common man would allow any writing or publishing, especially where extremely clandestine, to be any breach of the peace at all; and that none but lawyers, on account of the evil tendency sometimes of such writings, had first got them, by *construction* to be deemed so. I had no idea that it was possible for any lawyer, however subtle and metaphysical, to proceed so

far

far as to decide mere authorſhip, and publication by the preſs, to be an *actual* breach of the peace, as This laſt ſeemed to expreſs, *ex vi termini*, ſome poſitive bodily injury, or ſome immediate dread thereof at leaſt ; and that, whatever a challenge, in writing, to any particular might be, a general libel upon public meaſures, could never be conſtrued to be ſo. And I knew it was not required of any one in matters of law, to come up to the faith of an orthodox divine, who, in incredible points, is ready to ſay, *Credo quia impoſſibile eſt.*

Indeed, I had originally conceived, upon a much larger ſcale of reaſoning, that freedom from arreſt for a libel was a privilege incident and neceſſary to the Houſe of Commons, becauſe it was a ſafe-guard againſt the power of the Crown, in a matter that was almoſt always a diſpute between the miniſter and the ſubject, and no more than a natural ſecurity of perſon for an independent part of the legiſlature, againſt the arbitrary proceeding of a King's officer, in the leaſt aſcertained of all imputable offences. But this point has been lately cleared up to the contrary in St. Stephen's chapel, upon a debate of two ſucceſſive days, the laſt of which continued from three in the afternoon till two in the morning *. " And, I lament my not hearing a very long, refined and elaborate ſpeech of a certain candid lawyer, the product of family learning and patriotiſm ; nor the finer wove oration of a great juſticiary ; which have been highly celebrated and were made at different times and places, in order to eaſe peoples minds of ſuch chimæras as mine, and to convince the impartial part of mankind, that a libel is not only an actual breach of the peace, but ſcarcely diſtinguiſhable in a court-lawyer's underſtanding from treaſon itſelf." Nevertheleſs, the Commons of England at large, having come to no new compact or ſurrender of ancient privileges, ſtill poſſeſs their old right of being judges of the law in libel.

I cannot help adding too, with regard to pledges for good behaviour, that, in my apprehenſion, they are not demandable by law in the caſe of a libel, before conviction ; for this miſdemeanor is only made a breach of the peace at all, by political conſtruction, nothing being an actual

* Vide the printed Votes of Wedneſday the 23d of November 1763, and Thurſday the 24th of November, 1763.

breach

breach of the peace, but an assault or battery, the doing or attempting to do some bodily hurt. Now, surety for the peace is calculated as a guard from personal injury; and articles of the peace can only be demanded from a man, who by some positive fact has already broke the peace, and therefore is likely to do so again; or where any one will make positive oath, that he apprehends bodily hurt, or that he goes in danger of his life. The *articles* which are every day exhibited in the court of King's Bench, are always for the prevention of corporal damage. No case is so common as that of women exhibiting articles of the peace against their husbands; now, I do not believe, that if any wife was to allege, as a foundation for such articles her husband's having wrote a libel against her; let the libel be ever so false, scandalous and malicious; that Lord Mansfield would make the husband find sureties for the peace, or for his future good behaviour on that account. Another reason which strongly weighs with me is, that the writers upon bail, or the delivery of a man's person from prison, never mention sureties for the behaviour, in any case of a libel or constructive breach of the peace; and yet it would have been material for them so to have done, if such security must be given before a man could obtain his liberty. My Lord Coke has wrote an express treatise upon bail and mainprise, and considered the writs *de homine replegiando, de odio & atia,* and *Habeas Corpus,* and yet it is plain he had no imagination of the thing. He says, " Bail and mainprise is, when " a man detained in prison for any offence for which he " is bailable or mainprizable by law, is by a complete " Judge or Judges of that offence, upon sufficient sure- " ties, bound for his appearance and yielding of his body, " delivered out of prison. As for example, if a man be " indicted of any felonies, publishing of any seditious " books, &c. contrary to the form of an act made in " the 23d year of Queen Elizabeth, he may be bailed, " for the offence is made felony, and bail and mainprize " not prohibited." Now, in the case of a public libel, there is nobody who can come into the court of *King's Bench* and exhibit articles of the peace against the writer or publisher, swearing that he believes himself to be in danger of bodily hurt from him, and that he walks in fear of his life.

Besides,

Besides, for words scandalous in themselves or attended with consequential damages, or for a libel, the party traduced may bring an action of trespass on the case, which action however, lies only for a wrong done without force, but against the peace. Now, this must mean and can only be a *constructive* breach of the peace. For, if it were *an actual* breach of the peace, an action of trespass with force and arms would lie, as it does for an assault and battery and false imprisonment; but, I believe no lawyer ever heard of such an action being brought either for words, or for a libel, or would say that in either case it would lie. This therefore is a proof that the Law does not regard a mere libel as an *actual* breach of the peace.

It is further observable, that there is no adjudged case where this demand of surety for the peace in libel, has been determined to be legal; the crown hath in some cases, as in that of Mr. Amherst and others, after insisting upon it, avoided having the point determined, and relinquished the claim to it only on that account, and not till the last minute: it is contrary to the general principles and notions of law; and it may be the means of great oppression. Any gentleman would therefore serve his country, by resisting such a lawless demand, and by having it solemnly argued, upon the first occasion.

When a man is charged with a libel, by an arbitrary information *ex officio*, he must cry out, like a Roman of old, *Provoco ad Populum*; I appeal to my country, that is, to a Jury of my equals. I will give bail for my appearance to try the validity of this charge before them, but I will do nothing more. I never heard till very lately, that Attorney Generals, upon the caption of a man supposed a libeller, could insist upon his giving securities for his good behaviour. It is a doctrine injurious to the freedom of every subject, derogatory from the old constitution, and a violent attack, if not an absolute breach, of the liberty of the press. It is not law, and I will not submit to it.

What makes me insist the more upon all these points is, an assurance that the legal methods of proceeding in every case of a libel, are sufficiently severe, and that therefore all illegality is totally inexcusable. The prosecution is heavy, and if the supposed offender be found guilty by the Jury, his punishment may be extremely grievous.

After

After the trial, all the circumstances that appeared are reported, by the Judge who presided, to the *King's Bench*; and this Court gives judgment thereupon, after deliberation, and both can and will proportion the punishment to the case. They may, *after* conviction, pillory, fine, imprison, and even insist upon sureties for the good behaviour, according to the nature and degree, the mischievousness and tendency of the libel. In bad times, Sir Samuel Bernardiston, for letters not very extraordinary, was fined 10,000 l. In good times, Shebbeare, for the most seditious and treasonable libel that could be penned, was fined in no very great sum on account of his circumstances, but was pilloried, committed to prison for two years, and obliged to find security for his behaviour, in a pretty tolerable sum himself and two sureties in as much more, for seven years to come. All this may be done in the regular way of proceeding, and seems to be as much power of punishment as can be wanted, for a mere misdemeanor; because I presume nobody chuses to revert to the additional punishments inflicted before the Star-chamber was suppressed; such as public whippings, burning in the face, slitting the tongue and nostrils, cutting off the nose and ears, and long or perpetual imprisonment; which was the treatment of writers against Administrations in those days, and was absolutely inflicted at one time upon the three liberal professions, in the persons of a clergyman, a counsellor, and a physician.

If the libel be upon the Legislature, and the Libeller a Member, the House will expel him, as Queen Anne's Tories did Sir Richard Steele, for charging the Queen, and her Ministry, with a design of breaking the establishment and introducing the Pretender; and, yet, I suppose, now-a-days there is nobody who doubts in the least that Knight's having published the truth when he said so. Indeed, he admitted himself the Author of the paper complained of, so that the then Commons were not obliged to help that necessary fact out, by the reception of testimony not upon oath. Nay, the Courtiers of that day thought the punishment of expulsion alone so severe (although Sir Richard's creditors were not more numerous than Mr. Wilkes's) that they stopped there, and carried on no prosecution against him in Westminster Hall, or *any where else*.

D   I do

I do not touch again upon Mr. Wilkes in this place as commiserating him particularly, having ever avoided his acquaintance, but merely to say, what indeed the History of England from the beginning of the reign of Charles the First to the present time may illustrate, that prosecutions for libels generally arise from, and are pursued with a spirit of party-revenge. Men are upon such occasions apt to do things which in cooler moments they would be ashamed of. With respect to the last named Libeller, I must however declare, had I been his constant comrade, and my doors open to him at all hours, much more the partaker of his loosest pleasures, and of his most shameful blasphemies, I should not have stood forth, either in the one House or the other, as the immediate mover of *the poor devil's* public disgrace, censure, prosecution and ruin, or as the mercenary advocate of his pursuers; unless I had an inclination to convince mankind, that I was regardless of all principle whatever, excepting that of serving a party for my own private interest, and from that motive was willing to act upon any stage, the most inconsistent and most abandoned of all parts, even against the companions of my happiest moments; and to imprint this lesson upon the world, that no motive whatever of public good or private friendship was at the bottom of my conduct, or even the smaller restraint of common decorum. Real good-nature, friendliness, charity, (whatever you call it) will cover a multitude of sins, but mere companionable ease or mirth, with an unfeeling heart, only enhances the profligacy of a character. If debauchees will not sink below the worst of gangs, they should at least be true to each other, as kindred souls. In my own opinion, this ludicrous Libeller did himself all that his severest enemies could wish, to turn his own case into ridicule, and to let the people see that a love of farce and merriment predominated in all his actions; and that he had too much levity and viciousness of natural constitution, to make the good of his country the rule of his conduct in any one action of his life. But the sight of these very things should make grave men of all sides attend to the constitution in such contests of profligacy, to prevent the laws of their country from being made either the sport or the sacrifice of party upon the occasion. A point that is carried for the sake of punishing a worthless fellow, may be cited hereafter as a precedent for the most

dange-

dangerous prosecution and oppression of an excellent patriot.

The most respectful and constitutional of remonstrances from seven bishops, in behalf of the established religion, has been treated as a seditious libel, and nothing but the honesty of a Jury saved them from the most unjust condemnation. "The Attorney and Solicitor both affirmed "to James the 2d, That the honestest paper relating to "matters of civil government might be a seditious libel, "when presented by persons who had nothing to do with "such matters, as (they said) the Bishops had not but in "time of parliament *."

Mr. Somers's *modest plea for the Church of England*, underwent the same denomination, although it was no more than a seasonable defence of our national worship, upon the true principles of the constitution, against an arbitrary and Popish Court.

And I remember myself a tiny pamphlet, published by the Author of *The Considerations on the German war*, questioning the merits of the defence of Minorca, by argument, not by hard words or foul names, which was unfortunately on motion in the *King's Bench* deemed a libel, and an information in the ordinary way granted against the writer, whereby he became a considerable sufferer; and yet I believe any man who were to read this performance now, free from prejudice, would never concur in that opinion.

In short, one cannot guess what may, or may not, in some unlucky time, be regarded as a libel by some Judge or Attorney-general. The highest or lowest of Authors, the noblest or the most sneaking, the Original or the Copy, the Patriot or the Tool, the Head of a Party or the Amanuensis of a private Junto: in short, the most respectable Commonwealthsman or the paltriest of Coffee-house Listeners and Political Eavesdroppers, may equally chance to fall under this arbitrary brand.

Nay, if two foreigners here should happen to have a dispute relative to their respective characters or appointments, and a difference should arise about the œconomy or charges of one side and the other, and either should publish, by way of justification of his pretensions, letters that really

---

* See Lord Clarendon's State Letters, p. 317.

passed, they might, for aught I know, be held a libel, for which the Attorney-general might file an information, and whereto no defence, by the help of a little management, should be deemed possible, and which counsel might fairly give up without the loss of their character.

If a man was now to publish an ode, like that of Mr. Pulteney to Lord Lovel,

"Let's out for England's glory,"

inviting any courtier to join in measures of opposition to the administration, and it was to be written with half the spirit and beauty, it might be the object of an information *ex officio*, as a libel, altho' no man turned of thirty, I suppose, would think any placeman could be moved thereby to oppose the court, and quit a part of their finery, for the sake of being a patriot.

Nay, if it be law, that a man may be guilty of a libel by writing against the dead (as well as the living) I do not see how the world is ever to discuss the actions of administration, or any man to publish animadversions upon their conduct in particular instances; nor what is to become of the licensed historian, with his rule of *Nequid veri dicere non audeat*. For example, if I was to say of a late Great Chancellor, that I could not think he merited the appellation of a patriot, having ever regarded him as a decent, circumspect, prerogative lawyer; that he leaned in his notions too much towards aristocracy; that he seemed, in his politics, to approach much nearer to the principles of the Earl of Clarendon (whose title he once affected) than of Lord Somers; and that, at last, upon what *public* principles he joined the opposition, after having been in all things with the court for forty years before, I could never learn. It seemed, that even his opposition to, or rather disapprobation of, the peace, proceeded rather from a private dissatisfaction at the man who happened at last to have the making of it (his old friends being displaced) than from any motive of public concern; and some of his reasons against it, indifferent men thought the strongest in its behalf, namely the delineation of our boundary in North America, which, altho' the course of a great river is made to describe, he objected to, because its extremely distant *source* could neither be ascertained or denominated. His discourse, it was remarked, favoured more of a draughtsman arguing exceptions,

than

than of a statesman discussing a treaty. And nothing perhaps like it can be recollected, saving one equivocal speech of a similar texture, delivered in another place, but at the same time and upon the same occasion; where the arguments were so artificial, qualified and verbal, without edge or substance, that it would be extremely difficult to put into clear and distinct propositions, what was either affirmed or denied touching any of the articles themselves. Indeed, I could never determine whether he had, or had not, a good conception of our foreign interests, altho' I am persuaded he had a thorough one of all the domestic connections among us. I might add, that when a bill for a militia was presented, altho' he liked the name and speciously commended the design, yet he foresaw great difficulties and infinite danger in it, recalled to mens minds the public evils that followed from arms being put into the hands of the people, no less than the destruction of royalty and the suppression of peerage; and so found innumerable objections, both religious and political, to the form and the substance of the several clauses, and to all the regulations proposed. The tide, however, running for the measure, both as a national strength and a counterpoise to a standing army, he suggested several enervating amendments, to reduce the number proposed one half, and to have the other either officered wholly by the crown, or else unofficered at all, as a mere fund in the hands of the King, for the better supply of his standing army. The number was accordingly curtailed, and other qualifications took place. But, at last, when the bill became an act, things were so managed in his particular county, that the militia was never either embodied, or commuted for in money, in spite of the alternative laws for the purpose. He was apparently a principle man in, if not the sole cause of, defeating a new Habeas Corpus bill, passed unanimously by the Commons, and calculated for the prevention of some evasions of the old act: and that he projected, in concert with another new made peer, the marriage act, and, having disapproved a short bill drawn by the Judges, obliging people to marry in churches, that their marriages might be regularly registered and capable of proof; had the reputation of drawing another, filled with clauses calculated for the prevention of all marriages without consent, with a view, as it should seem, to per-

petuate

petuate, as much as might be, a fortune or family once made, by continuing, from generation to generation, a vast power of property, and to facilitate at each descent, the lumping of one great sum, or one great family, to another, by bargain and sale, in opposition to the generous principles of equality and diffusive property, which free states have always encouraged. The royal family, however, was excepted out of this late act, altho' their marriages are alone an object of public concern or influence. I might ask too, whether his Lordship did not uniformly throughout his life pursue his own private interest, and raise the greatest fortune, and provide the most amply for his family, of any lawyer that ever lived; and whether, during his dominion, the judicial promotions were disposed of upon ministerial motives, or merely agreeable to professional desert. I might nevertheless, and ought to add, that the same illustrious personage was blessed with a good temper, and great worldly prudence, which are the two hand-maids in ordinary to prosperity; that his whole deportment was amiable; and that he possessed, in general, the soundest understanding in matters of law and equity, and the best talents for judicature I had ever seen; that he might be cited as an example, in this country, of the perfect picture of a good Judge, which my Lord Bacon hath so admirably drawn; and that he was, in short, a truly wise magistrate. He was free from the levities, vices and expences, which are so commonly the product of a lively and prurient fancy. His station did not require, nor his genius furnish him with imagination, wit or eloquence. And, perhaps, had he possessed a true taste for the fine arts and the politer parts of literature, he would never have been so extensive a lawyer, to which, however, the plainness of his education might have somewhat contributed. In short, one might say that, Lord Somers and He seem to have been the reverse of each other in every respect.

Now, this might be prosecuted as a libel on the dead; whereas, the writer penned no part of it maliciously, nor falsely as he believed, and did not mention a tenth part of what he might, in support of the justness of the character. And therefore, unless a matter be thoroughly canvassed, and gentlemen at the bar will speak out to a Jury, that they may have the proper information to deliberate upon,

it

it is hard to say what may not very glibly pass at one time or other for a libel. Every thing seems to depend upon the Jury's considering and determining both the law and the fact.

I trust, therefore, this singular privilege will ever be exercised by the people themselves. If they once give it up, they will never know any thing of public transactions, but from the most partial and least credited of all mankind, from writers employed by the authors of the measures themselves, who, like Scotch Reviewers, may have the face to attempt to make Englishmen believe, that a man can be a constitutional judge who quits the laws of the land and deviates from the established practice of courts, in spight of common sense and the constant declaration of our ancestors, *nolumus leges Angliæ mutari*. Let the dependent judges before the Revolution have advanced what doctrine they please, the *fact* has been, that juries have always exercised the right of determining what is a libel. It hath saved this constitution often, is the great bulwark of liberty, and should never be resigned, but with the last breath.

Few men know much of the nature of polity, and, of them, all do not sufficiently attend to the conduct of Administration, to observe when slight innovations are made in the laws or in their Administration; and, of those who do, very few indeed have that degree of understanding which enables them to judge soundly of the consequences of such alterations, with respect to their liberties in general. Again; of these very few, not more than one perhaps, has activity, resolution and public spirit enough to publish his thoughts (as Mr. Somers did upon several occasions) concerning what was going forward, in order to alarm (like a good citizen) the rest of his fellow subjects. Insomuch, that breaches in the constitution, which by degrees bring on a total loss of liberty, are either wholly unnoticed, or else are regarded as the mere violences of party, by which nobody can be affected but the immediate actors. Whereas, for the sake of compassing their own ends, there is nothing which party-men will not do, *per fas aut nefas*; just as an established high churchman will persecute even to death, any other man or divine that questions his authority or his doctrine. From hence arise precedents of all sorts of illegal and unconstitutional

tutional practices. Ministers (as not one in a thousand is actuated by any principle of public good, or even by a desire of honest fame) for the sake of power, title, riches, and pre-eminence of any kind, will deceive the best inclined Prince, and minister to the humour, folly, vices, and domination of the worst. On the Exclusion-bill, no more than two, even of the Bishops, would venture to vote for it, altho' their Bishopricks depended upon the continuance of the Protestant religion, which that bill was avowedly framed to preserve. Now, when an impartial man gathers this, both from his own experience and from history, how can he help being moved at the doctrine that is publicly held with respect to writings that animadvert upon public proceedings, and the use that is made of that desperate sword, an information, together with the means which are every day devised to make it more dreadful?

I will venture to prophesy, that if the reigning notions concerning libels be pushed a little farther, no man will dare to open his mouth, much less to use his pen, against the worst Administration that can take place, however much it behoves the people to be apprized of the condition they are likely to be in. In short, I do not see what can be the issue of such law, but an universal acquiescence to any men or any measures, that is, a downright passive obedience.

There is one great reason, why every patriot should wish this sort of writings to be encouraged; which is, that animadversions upon the conduct of ministers, submitted to the eye of the public in print, must in the nature of the thing be a great check upon their bad actions, and, at the same time, an incentive to their doing of what is praiseworthy. Nevertheless, if it be once clear law, That a paper may be a libel, whether true or false, written against a good, or bad man, when alive or dead, who is there that may not continue a Minister, whether he has a grain of honesty or understanding, if he should happen to be a Favourite at Court? The worse his actions are, the more truly and sharp the writer states them; and the more the public, from his just reasonings, detest and cry out against them, the more scandalous and seditious, of course, will be the libel; for, *the truth of the fact is an aggravation* of the libel; and it was That which occasioned the clamour. There is but one step farther

ther before you arrive at complete despotism, and that is to extend the same doctrine to words spoken, and This I am persuaded would in truth very soon follow. And then what a blessed condition should we all be in! when neither the liberty of free writing or free speech, about every body's concern, about the management of public money, public law and public affairs, was permitted; and every body was afraid to utter what every body however could not help thinking!

With respect to libels on a particular person, in his private capacity, there may be some little foundation for a doctrine of this sort; because, as the welfare of the State has nothing to do with his private transactions, you ought not to make reflections which may injure him in his calling or his reputation; you must always do this out of personal spite, and therefore ought to be punished for such your malevolence.

But, the case is totally different with respect to an Administration; for the country in general is always the better or the worse for its conduct, and therefore every man has a right to know, to consider, and to reflect upon It. Their posts in the State, or their public characters, are not like any individual's particular trade, profession or fortune or his private character. The writing of them out of their places in the Government is not a loss for which they have any right to be repaired in damages. Their holding ought only to be *quam diu bene se gesserint*, and of this the people at large ought to be made judges, as every man in this country is represented, and consequently concerned in the legislature itself.

However, from a confusion of these two different kinds of libels, introduced and upheld from very bad motives, it seems to me that a general doctrine has been laid down. Now, my notion is, that in public libels the truth of the charge should be an absolute defence, whatever may be thought necessary with regard to private libels. The public is essentially interested in this discrimination being made.

When men find themselves aggrieved by the violence or the misconduct of the persons appointed to the Ministry, it is natural for them to complain, to communicate their thoughts to others, to put their neighbours on their guard, and to remonstrate in print against the public proceedings.

E They

They have a right ſo to do, as much as a borough has a right to reject any Court candidate, and to publiſh the reaſons for ſo doing; and both of theſe rights will I hope be exerciſed until there can be both a congè de dire and d'ecrire, and a congè d'elire, eſtabliſhed in the State as there already is in the church. The liberty of expoſing and oppoſing a bad Adminiſtration by the pen, is among the neceſſary privileges of a free people, and is perhaps the greateſt benefit that can be derived from the liberty of the preſs. But Miniſters, who by their miſdeeds provoke the people to cry out and complain, are very apt to make that very complaint the foundation of a new oppreſſion, by proſecuting the ſame as a libel on the State. Now, the merit or demerit of theſe publications muſt ariſe from their being true or falſe; if they are true, they are highly commendable; if they are wilfully falſe, they are certainly malicious, ſeditious and damnable. The mere pretence of a paper being ſeditious, if the matter of it be fact, is to be diſregarded; for, I do not ſee how any writer can publiſh to the world the juſteſt and moſt important complaints, without tending thereby to render the people and their conſtituents diſſatisfied with the adminiſtration, and even clamorous againſt it. Nay, I ſcarcely can frame to myſelf any other way of letting his Majeſty know that the miniſtry he has appointed is bad. However, if a miniſter notwithſtanding ſhould continue a favourite at court, and the people being affected with what was written ſhould clamor, and have great reaſon for ſo doing, I make no doubt but any Attorney-general, upon the ſlighteſt hint from the proper place, would file an information againſt the Writer, and charge him at once with endeavouring to alienate the affections of the people, and to raiſe *traitorous* inſurrections againſt the peace of the King; altho' it were obvious to every indifferent perſon, that the unlucky writer had no ſuch intention, nay, had been ready on a former occaſion voluntarily to aſſociate for the defence of his Majeſty's title; and to venture his life in the field to ſupport it. And yet I am fully convinced, that were it not for ſuch writings as have been proſecuted by Attorney-generals for libels, we ſhould never have had a Revolution, nor his preſent Majeſty a regal Crown; nor ſhould we now enjoy a proteſtant religion, or one jot of civil liberty. Kings can hardly receive any intelligence but what their miniſters give

give them, and thefe gentlemen, being generally guided by avarice and ambition, endeavour to reprefent every man who ftrives to get them difmiffed from their employs, as one who is about to attack the throne itfelf, call him traitor directly, and then exert the power of the crown to demolifh him. The ufe of the word *treafonable* is generally, in my confcience, to give them a pretence for difregarding the common rules of Law and Juftice. And if they are queftioned in parliament for what they have done, they are in hopes a majority may be procured to come to a refolution in their favor, or at worft, to prevent any from being come to againft them. And then, who dares fay they have done amifs?

Libels are by no means a " harmlefs fport"; for truth alone can excufe any man in complaining even of a bad magiftrate: but yet, I cannot think them fuch dreadful things as vindicate minifters in breaking through every law for the fake of coming at the writer. I believe moft fober men, who fee already what lengths fuch profecutions may be carried according to law, and how deeply the liberties of the people may be affected by fuch means, are of opinion, that if fome of the legal methods of profecution now acquiefced in were done away, the conftitution would be the better for it. The prerogative which an Attorney-general affumes of filing an information againft whomfoever he pleafes, is certainly a reproach to a free people; and if the regular information awarded upon fpecial motion by the *King's Bench* were likewife taken away, I do not think the conftitution would be injured by it: in which cafe, the old common law method of indicting for a libel, as a violation of the peace, would be the means that every body muft refort to; and in my own opinion a grand jury [*] are very competent and the propereft judges, whether any publication be deftructive to the welfare of the ftate or not.

Altho' there is as yet no licenfing act afoot, except for the Stage; if a man prints what is fuppofed libellous, either on the ftate, or any particular perfon, he is liable to be profecuted for it. But people like to fee a profecution go forward in the ordinary way, as was the cafe with Dr.

---

[*] See a valuable treatife upon Grand Juries called *The Security of Englifhmen's Lives*, attributed to Mr. Somers, who not only underftood the conftitution but loved it.

Shebbeare: in comparison with whose writings, those of Mr. Wilkes may really be said to be " a mere exercise of wit and talents, and an innocent exertion of the liberty of the press." Mankind will ever dislike violent proceedings. Altho' the person himself may merit the chastisement he meets with, yet if this be inflicted by illegal methods, it will make every man fear, should he raise the resentment of the ministry, that himself would be treated in like manner, whether he had committed any crime in law or not. If things are done in one instance contrary to law, they may in another. No man is secure, when the laws of the land cease to be a protection. Although the messenger, or the dragoon, be not at my door, yet it is very disheartening to find that it is no longer in my power to be secure against their being there. My liberty is equally gone.

No necessities of state can ever be a reason for quitting the road of law in the pursuit of a libeller. The attack of this class of writers seldom goes farther than the minister, for the sake of bringing in some other man; and so far from being " of all other the instance the most dangerous to the public quiet", is certainly not at all so, if by the public quiet be meant the establishment itself.

The notion of pursuing a libeller in a *criminal* way at all, is alien from the nature of a free constitution. Our antient common law knew of none but a *civil* remedy, by special action on the case for damages incurred, to be assessed by a jury of his fellows. Indeed, the doctrine in courts of law used to be, that " no writing whatever is " to be esteemed a libel, unless it reflect upon some par- " ticular person." There was no such thing as a public libel known to the law. In order, however, to gratify some of the great men, in the weak reign of Richard the 2d, some acts of parliament were passed to give actions for false tales, news, and slander of peers or certain great officers of state; which are now termed *de scandalis magnatum*. Before that time, or at most the 3 Edward 1. ho mere words were actionable, unless some special damage thereby was alleged and proved. Even now-a-days, the courts of common law will not sustain actions for mere obscene discourses by word of mouth or writing, or for ribaldry. They leave such spiritual concerns to the ecclesiastical censures of courts christian. And it is very

notorious

notorious from history, that the most sanctified and pharisaical ministries and reigns, when the church has been founded the most, have been the most corrupt and slavish.

The whole doctrine of libels, and the criminal mode of prosecuting them by information, grew with that accursed court the star-chamber. All the learning intruded upon us *de libellis famosis* was borrowed at once, or rather translated, from that slavish imperial law, usually denominated the civil law. You find nothing of it in our books higher than the time of Q. Elizabeth and Sir Edward Coke.

But, if any writing should be a libel, and be prosecuted only as such, it is in vain afterwards to call it "abominable or treasonable," with any idea that such epithets will warrant an extraordinary proceeding in the prosecutor. This end indeed it may answer, and a very diabolical one it is; it may serve to found a pretence for demanding excessive bail, which if the supposed libeller cannot find, he must lie in prison: however, as there have several acts of parliament passed from time to time forbidding excessive bail, particularly the Habeas Corpus act, and as the House of Commons have even since in the case of Lord Chief Justice Scroggs expressed their detestation of such oppression, a Judge is not now so likely to put this mode of tyranny in use. But if the doctrine of security for the peace can be established, I do not see what should hinder a time-serving magistrate, from insisting upon ever so enormous a pledge *eo nomine:* The Judge might say, I have taken moderate bail ; but, I found he was a man of parts, much dis-inclined to his Majesty's measures of administration, and had reason to think he would still write against them, which could not fail of raising a dangerous sedition; and therefore I thought the best way was to take such a pledge for his good behaviour for seven years, as would deter him from writing any thing that could possibly be deemed a libel ; for if he did, he would forfeit his caution-money, and That would be so great a loss, it would absolutely ruin him. I did for the best ; and, I do not know that there is any statute which prescribes any measure for security of the peace. Now, supposing a chief Justice was to be complained of for such an oppression, as a gross fraud on the spirit and intention of the Habeas Corpus act, and the

House

House of Commons were to inquire into the matter; if the administration which he served was then prevalent, it might perhaps be very difficult to obtain any censure of the practice; but, if that could be done, it is highly improbable they would go any farther; and, at the worst, his Lordship would get off without any fine upon himself, as well as Chief Justice Scroggs did. To say the truth, and to speak out upon so material a subject, I cannnt help imagining that this word *treasonable* or *traitorous*, is frequently thrown into the charge against a supposed libeller by an Attorney General, for the purpose of affording colour for the demand of high bail, and, if possible, enormous security for the good behaviour.

Had this practice of surety for the peace upon the charge of a libel prevailed in Charles the IId's time, it is inconceivable that the legislature should not have mentioned it by name in the Habeas Corpus act. The patriots who procured that statute, evidently meant to have a delivery of the body in all cases not capital by bail, and must certainly think by the words *speedy relief of all persons imprisoned for criminal or supposed criminal matters*, that they had provided for all cases of misdemeanor.

It is no excuse for this novel attempt to say, that Judges take the same sureties for appearance and for the peace, and make the one the measure of the other; because they are certainly not obliged so to do, and might perhaps on some occasion see reason to do otherwise; besides, a man might forfeit his pledges for the behaviour by some subsequent imprudence, altho' he might be acquitted of the charge which had occasioned them, and this could never be the intention of any legislature.

In speaking of sureties, I have not entered into the difference between those for the *peace*, and for the *good behaviour*; but the latter are certainly by much the most to be dreaded. For " surety of the peace cannot be broken
" without some *act*, as an affray or battery, or the like.
" Whereas (according to my Lord Coke) surety *de bono*
" *gestu*, or good abearing, consists chiefly in that a man
" demean himself well in his port and company, doing
" nothing that may be *cause* of the breach of the peace,
" or of putting the people in fear or trouble." In short, it affords more room for a latitude of construction, or for a

Judges

Judges discretion, which is very apt to operate against the subject, and should therefore be studiously avoided.

The truth is, at common law, surety for the good behaviour could be demanded in no case before conviction by a jury. Binding to the good behaviour was a discretionary judgment, given by a court of record, for an offence at the suit of the King, after a verdict; trial by his peers being an Englishman's birth-right in all charges, not to be taken away but by act of parliament.

"Originally, wardens or conservators of the peace, were wont to be elected in the full county before the sheriff; they had only co-ertion or prehension in a few cases, and no jurisdiction in any cause.

"But, when young Edward the 3d, by the means of his mother and Sir Roger Mortimer, had forcibly got possession of his father's crown, He instituted keepers, commissioners, or justices of the peace, as so many special eyes and watches over the common people, whereby the election of conservators of the peace was taken from the people, and translated to the assignment of the King. These justices were not ordained however, to reduce the people to an universal unanimity, but to suppress injurious force and violence against the person, his goods or possessions. In this matter of the peace (continues Mr. Lambard) the law of God respects the mind and conscience, the laws of men do look but to the body, hands and weapons: and therefore, furious gesture and beastly force of body (and not every contention, suit and disagreement of minds) is the proper subject about which the office of the justices of the peace is to be exercised."

Before the 2d of Edward 3, justices could only report to the parliament; but, by that statute, they had power to punish disobeyers and resisters. And the 34th of the same King enacts, "that in every county shall be assigned for the keeping of the peace one Lord, and with him three or four of the most worthy in the county, with some learned in the law, and they shall have power to *restrain misfeasors*, rioters, and all other barrators, and to pursue, arrest, take and chastise them, according to their trespass and offence; and to cause them to be imprisoned and duly punished, according to the law and customs of the realm; and also to inform of
them;

"them; and to inquire of all those that have been pil-
"lors and robbers in the parts beyond the sea, and be
"now come again, and go wandring, and will not
"labor as they were wont; and to take and arrest all
"those that they may find by indictment, or by suspicion,
"and to put them in prison; and to take *of all them
"that be not of good fame*, where they shall be found,
"*sufficient surety and mainprize of their good behaviour*
"towards the King and his people, and the other duly
"*to punish*, *to the intent* that the people be not by *such
"rioters or rebels*, troubled nor endamaged, nor the peace
"blemished, *nor merchants nor others passing by the high-
"ways* disturbed, nor put in the *peril* which may hap-
"pen of *such* offenders." Now, it is plain, this statute
regards nothing but actual offenders, rioters, barrators,
rebels and highwaymen: and surety for the behaviour cannot be taken thereby, but of those who are on strong
ground suspected of some such actual breach of the peace.
This law, nevertheless, is the origin and the sole foundation
for the present demand of sureties for the good behaviour
before conviction; and what is not warranted by the
provisions of this act, is illegal and unwarrantable, the common law permitting no such thing, and the same being in
itself derogatory of the rights of a freeman.

Indeed, some particular statutes in subsequent reigns,
have directed surety for the good Abearing in cases therein
specified; as the 1st Mary, for disturbing a preacher, or
irreverent handling the sacrament, altar or crucifix; the
5th Eliz. for taking of fish in ponds or deer in parks; the
23d Eliz. for absenting for 12 months from church;
the 39th Eliz. for disturbing the execution of that statute,
either for the punishment of rogues, or for the relief or
setting on work of the poor; and the 3d James for unlaw-
fully hunting and stealing deer or conies, &c. But, these
special statutes are out of the present question, and therefore need not be touched upon here.

To return then to the 34th Ed. 3. It appears (I think)
uncontrovertibly from the penning of that statute, as
well as from the acceptation of it among our ancestors,
and the construction of antient lawyers, that security for
good behaviour cannot be required, but where a man shews
just cause to apprehend some bodily hurt to be done to himself. And in such case, the peace-magistrate must con-
vene

vene the person charged, *inquire* and *find* him not to be of good fame where taken. He must examine into the truth of the matter alleged, try and adjudge it upon satisfactory testimony or evidence of the thing, unless he saw it with his own eyes, before he can legally demand any surety for good abearing, or know what to take: for, he acts judicially. In short, mainprize for the behaviour, (whether by bond to the King, pledge or caution) must be by a regular proceeding of record. In fact, none but a judge of record (which a justice of peace is) can take a recognizance, because the acknowlegement of the sum is to remain as a matter of record. Every recognizance for the peace is expresly directed by the 3d Henry 7, to be certified to the next sessions. And, before the reign of James I, it was not imagined that security for the behaviour could be taken by one justice, and all the books in his time recommend two. Nay, binding to the behaviour, used always to be done in open sessions; and the best opinions now are, that a justice acts illegally, if he bind any man to his behaviour for any longer time than untill the next sessions of the peace. My Lord Hale says, " This binding, tho' expressed generally, and with-
" out any time limited, is not intended to be perpetual,
" but in nature of bail, viz. to appear at such a day at
" the sessions, and *in the mean time* to be of good be-
" haviour."

Indeed, by supplicavit from the Chancery or King's Bench, a justice may be commanded to take surety for the good abearing, of any particular person; and then in obedience to the writ he must do so, for he acts only ministerially. The supreme courts, however, are commanded by " the 21st James I, to grant no process of the peace
" for good behaviour, but upon motion in open court,
" and declaration in writing and upon oath, to be ex-
" hibited by the party desiring such process, of the causes
" for which such process shall be granted; the motion
" and declaration to be mentioned on the back of the
" writ; and if it shall afterwards appear that the causes
" are untrue, the court may order *costs to the party*
" *grieved*, and commit the offender till paid." This act is professedly by its preamble made to prevent surety for the behaviour being unjustly " procured upon oaths pe-
" remptorily and corruptly taken and upon false sugges-
" tions

' tions and surmises," which shews that it is only to be awarded after a solemn examination into the truth of the cause suggested, upon strong and satisfactory evidence, in open court, in the face of mankind.

What then must one think of any court of justice that shall, upon the caption of a man as a libeller, refuse to let him to bail before he has entered likewise into recognizance for his behaviour, and even that without limit of time? An aspiring Attorney-general, at the instigation of a peevish and suspicious minister, may charge any paper as a libel, and any man as the author or publisher *ex officio*, without oath or the shadow of legal proof! The information may be filed, process taken out and executed, and the supposed libeller obliged to become bound in a heavy sum for his good behaviour, without stint of time; and yet the information may never be tried, or withdrawn, nor the recognizance released! Nay, if the same person should afterwards be guilty of any petty constructive misdemeanor or breach of the peace, it might be pretended that he had forfeited his former heavy recognizance; so that he would be punished, not in proportion to his real transgression, but to one that was only supposed; and this in a country where the law presumes every man to be innocent until he be found guilty! In plain words, it is a libel on the constitution to hold such doctrine, and in a judge, a breach of his trust (not to say high treason) to support it. It would render every English subject, by possibility, a most miserable fettered slave. Mr. Selden knew well the contrary, and therefore suffered himself to be re-imprisoned rather than submit to so lawless a demand of the crown, as that of surety for his behaviour, and thus in his own person to afford a precedent or sanction, for what might afterwards be attempted against others of his fellow-subjects. He was a great lawyer and a true representative of the people in parliament, in opposition to the tyrannical procedure of an arbitrary court and its subservient judges, that would have held every man *in misericordia regis*, if they could.

Having seen what the words of the statute, creating this power are; let us now look at the commission for the peace framed in consequence of it: premising that no usage, royal proclamation, or exposition of a judge, will make law in this case, that is not warranted by the express

words

words of the statute, and that the same being a penal statute it must be construed strictly.

The clause in the old commission of justices of the peace, authorizing them to take surety of the peace or good behaviour, confines the same to actual breaches of the peace, that is, threats of bodily injury or the burning of their habitations, and is in these words, " ad omnes " illos qui alicui de populo nostro de *corporibus suis*, vel " de *incendio domorum* suarum *minas fecerint*, ad suffi- " cientem securitatem de pace vel de bono gestu, erga " nos & populum nostrum, inveniendam, &c." And the words settled in James the 1st's time and now pursued, are, " To keep, and cause to be kept, all ordinances and " statutes for the good of the peace, &c. and to chastise " and punish all persons that offend, according to the form " of those statutes and ordinances; and to cause to come " before you all those, who to any of our people *con-* " *cerning their bodies*, or the *firing of their houses, have used* " *threats*, to find sufficient security for the peace or their " good behaviour, towards us and our people; and, if " they shall refuse to find such security, then them in our " prisons until the shall find such security to cause to be " *safely kept*. We have also assigned you to *inquire the* " *truth more fully* by the oath of good and lawful men, " &c. of all those in companies against our peace, in dis- " turbance of our people, have gone or rode, or here- " after shall presume to go or ride; and also of all those " who have there lain in wait, or hereafter shall pre- " sume to lie in wait, to maim or cut or kill our people."

Now, this commission is grounded evidently on the statute of Edward the 3d, derives its force from it, and needs no comment to apply thereto the several parts of it. It confirms abundantly the doctrine I have advanced. Indeed, the legality of requiring surety of good behaviour for Arson, seems very questionable, as not comprized within the act. However, nobody will object to it, as being a security against being burnt in one's bed, by any man who shall threaten, or by lurking about the house at night shall indicate an intention of so doing. It is most certain, nevertheless, that surety for the peace or the be-- haviour could be demanded in no case whatever at com-- mon law, before conviction, that it springs wholly from statute law within time of memory, and that the statute authorizes it only in cases of real personal danger; wherefore it may very well be doubted upon what legal bottom it can be extended farther. In the reign of Edward the 4th, it was determined, that it ought not to be granted to a man who shall demand it because he is in fear that another will take and imprison him; by reason that he may have a writ de homine replegiando, or an action of false imprisonment whereby he may be repaired in damages. This may be too strict a construction. But it is a proof that our ancestors thought the statute ought to be strictly construed, and that surety of the behaviour was only to be had as a protection from bodily maiming or destruction, indicated and proved by threats of immediate injury, by the wear of dangerous and forbidden arms, or by wandring and lurking about highways, and other suspicious places, in a suspected manner. It has been resolved that this security cannot be demanded for fear of harm to servants, cattle, or goods; altho' a servant may demand it for himself in his own person like any other man: and it is never to be awarded by any magistrate but upon credible oath, or upon his own view, of a sufficient cause. My Lord Coke says expresly, that " slanderous words are not a " breach of the behaviour, for tho' such words are mo-" tives and *mediate* provocations for breach of the peace, " yet tend they not *immediately* to a breach of the peace " like a challenge, &c." Many strange discretionary deviations, however, from the words of the statute, have been made and upheld with forced constructions by judges, in the flux of time; untill, in the latter end of James the 1st's reign, it came to be asserted by Mr. Dalton, in his book, that surety for the behaviour could be demanded of libellers. I presume, however, he must mean for such a libel on some particular person as directly and immediately tends to provoke him to fight; for, I believe, it has been reserved to our day, and to the compilement of crown-law by Serjeant Hawkins, to have it maintained either in print or at the bar, that such surety can be required for any public libel, or for a libel on any particular person not directly tending to an immediate breach of the peace. Be this as it may, the position is not warranted by any act of parliament, and is therefore absolutely illegal.

It has been resolved " That sedition cannot be committed by words, but by public and violent action." And my Lord Coke himself (the introductor, fosterer, maturer and reporter of the present star-chamber doctrine about libels) relates " that in the 30th of Q. Elizabeth, one King with sureties was bound by recognizance to appear at the *next* sessions and *in the mean time* to be of the good behaviour. That he appeared and was indicted for slanderous words spoken," *since his binding*, to a squire, namely, *Thou art a pelter, a lyar, and has told my Lord stories,* and for *breaking and entring the squire's close and chasing and vexing his cattle,* and for calling him afterwards *a drunken knave.* That the indictment was removed afterwards into the King's Bench, and there it was debated divers times both at the bar and the bench; whether, admitting all that is contained in the indictment to be true, any thing therein was in judgment of law a breach of the said recognizance. And that it was resolved " neither any of the words, nor the trespass were any breach of the good behaviour, for that none of them did tend immediately to the breach of the peace, for tho' the words *liar and drunken knave* are provocations, yet tend they not immediately to the breach of the peace, as if King had challenged the squire to fight with him, or had threatened to beat or wound him, or the like, for these tend immediately to the breach of the peace, to a trespass on the person, and therefore are breaches of the recognizance of the good behaviour."

" Surety of the peace also (according to some great authorities) is not to be granted, but where there is a fear of some present, or future danger, and not merely for a trespass or battery, or any breach of the peace that is *past*; for, this sort of surety is only for the security of such as are *in fear.*"

Dr. *Burn*, after giving a succinct and clear history of the several extensions of the sense of the statute, case after case, and reign after reign, with striking propriety remarks, that " one great inlet, to the larger and at length almost unlimited interpretation of the words, was an adjudication in Henry the Seventh's time, That it was lawful to arrest a man for the good behaviour, for haunting a suspected bawdy-house, with women of *bad fame*;"
and

and concludes with the following judicious reflections. "Thus the sense of this statute has been extended, not only to offences immediately relating to the peace, but to divers misbehaviour not directly tending to a breach of the peace; insomuch, as it is become difficult to define how far it shall extend, and where it shall stop. Therefore, the natural and received sense of any statute ought not to be departed from without extreme necessity; for, one concession will make way for another, and the latter will plead for the same right of admission as the former."

Let the legislature interpose therefore, when they shall think fit, and see the public safety requires it; but, I hope, no crown Judge will ever presume, for the future, to do more than *jus dicere*, and not dare *jus dare*. Every day makes one more sensible of the wisdom of *Aristotle*'s counsel in making laws " *Quoad ejus* fieri possit, quamplurima " *legibus ipsis* definiantur, quam paucissima *judicis arbitrio* " relinquantur." If Judges are not bound fast with chains of *laws, customs, ordinances and statutes*, it is impossible to divine what a servile Chief Justice may not one day give out for law, to gratify the spleen of an anxious, conscience-stung, and detected minister.* And such a horror have I, particularly, of the introduction of any new *criminal* law into this country, that, were it to happen, rather than submit thereto, I should be even for accompanying a noble Law-lord to *Ultima Thule*, which, by the shiver he spoke it with, I guess must be Scotland, the very northern scrag or bleakest barebone of the island. A man would fly any where in such case.

When the Archbishop of Canterbury and six other Bishops were called into the Council-chamber by James the 2d, and only pressed to enter into a recognizance, "They said, they were informed that no man was obliged to enter into recognizance, unless there were special matter against him, and that there was oath of it made against that person; and at last they insisted there was no precedent that any member of the House of Peers should be bound in recognizance *for misde-*

---

* Whoever is inclined to enter fully into this important part of the law, *Surety for the behaviour*, should consult Marrow, Crompton, Lambard's Eirenarchy, Pulton de Pace, Fitzherbert's and Burn's Justice, &c.

" *meanor*.

" *meanor.* The Lord Chancellor (Jeffreys) said there
" were precedents for it; but being desired to name one,
" he named none. Thereupon the Archbishop declared
" he had the advice of the best council, and they had
" warned him of this." Let me ask then, whether the
privilege of parliament is greater in one house than in the
other?

Whether the warrant of Lord H. was only for a seditious
or for a seditious and treasonable libel, makes no difference.
The fact indeed is, that the * warrant, which was for
apprehending persons and papers, does not mention the word
libel at all, but uses the terms, *a seditious and treasonable
paper;* and the second ** warrant, which was for committing Mr. Wilkes to the Tower, makes use of the
terms, *a most infamous and seditious libel.* So that there
is a diversity of denomination and description observed by
the drawer of the warrant, whether the same were the
Secretary of state, his law clerk, or the solicitor to the
treasury. Then comes the Attorney General, who files
his

---

* George Montagu Dunk Earl of Halifax, Viscount Sunbury and Baron Halifax, one of the Lords of his Majesty's most honourable Privy Council, *Lieutenant General of his Majesty's forces,* and principal Secretary of State.

These are in his Majesty's Name to authorize and require you (taking a constable to your assistance) to make strict and diligent search for the authors, printers and publishers of a seditious and treasonable paper intitled the North Briton Numb. 45. Saturday April 22, 1763, printed for G. Kearsly in Ludgate-street, London, and them, or any of them, having found, to apprehend or seize together with their papers, and to bring in safe custody before me, to be examined concerning the premisses and further dealt with according to law. And in the due execution thereof, all Mayors, Sheriffs, Justices of the Peace, Constables and all other his Majesty's Officers civil and *military,* and loving subjects whom it may concern are to be aiding and assisting to you, as there shall be occasion, and for so doing this shall be your warrant. Given at St. James's the 26th day of April, in the 3d year of his Majesty's reign.

Dunk Halifax.

To Nathan Carrington, John Money, James Watson and Robert Blackmore.

** Charles Earl of Egremont and George Dunk Earl of Halifax, Lords of his Majesty's most Honourable Privy Council and principal Secretaries of State.

These are in his Majesty's name to authorize and require you to receive into your custody the body of John Wilkes, Esq; herewith sent you for being the author and publisher of a most infamous and seditious libel, intitled, the North Briton, Number 45; tending to inflame the minds and alienate the affections of the people from his Majesty, and to excite them to traitorous
insur-

his information *ex officio* against the writer, and *charges* him with writing a libel. Now, *he* certainly knows what he is about, whether the others did or not; and therefore there is no longer any room for dispute about the crime, it is ascertained. Indeed, the King's message * to the House, delivered by the *Chancellor of the Exchequer* touching the same paper, calls it no more than a most seditious and dangerous libel, and the Resolution of the Commons execrates it but as a false, scandalous and seditious libel.

But a decisive argument upon this head is, that had the charge been other than a misdemeanor, it could not have been prosecuted in this way; for, no *information* will lie for a capital crime, or for misprision of treason. The statute says, it shall not lie for life or limb.

It is childish therefore to ask, whether the printing of any particular libel, as for instance, of the North Briton N°. 45, " is to be considered as no higher an offence than publishing a libel?" The Attorney says, " had it been " adjudged to have excited, instead of tending to excite, " it would have been no less a crime against the State, " than that of high treason, without any palliation whatever:" to which I can only say in a plain way, that had it been adjudged to have been something else than a libel, it would not have been adjudged what it was; for, I do not know that any law-logic ever proved *libel* and *high treason* to be convertible terms. No two offences can be more distinct in their nature or kind. One is *by construction*, a breach of the peace, and the other is the highest of all capital crimes, by express statute.

To compass or to imagine (that is to excite to, or intend) the death of the King, is High Treason, and is punished

---

insurrections against the government. And to keep him safe and *close*, until he shall be delivered by due course of law; for so doing this shall be your warrant. Given at St. James's the 30th day of April, 1763, in the 3d year of his Majesty's reign.

Egremont.
Dunk Halifax.

To the Right Honourable Lord John Berkeley of Stratton, Constable of his Majesty's Tower of London, or to the Lieutenant of the said Tower or his Deputy.

* Vide the Printed Votes of Tuesday Nov. 15. 1763.

nished with loss of life, by hanging, drawing and quartering, whether the King be killed, or even hurt or not. But this doctrine holds in no other crime whatever. For, in petty treason, which is the next greatest crime that the law knows, and which is the murder of a husband by the wife, or of the master by the servant, the inciting of others to perpetrate the fact, or any attempt to do it oneself, without effect, is only punishable as a misdemeanor and as an assault. Let us not then be so impudently imposed upon as to be told, that every step we take in questioning the acts of a minister, is high treason. Every London or Westminster mob, every riot, every abuse of administration or of a party; every remark or animadversion upon a proclamation, or upon a speech from the throne, or, in short, upon any other public measure of the ministry will in this way of reasoning soon be deemed Treason, to the disgrace of ourselves, the dishonour of our constitution, and the loss of the rights of a free people.

In truth, I likewise suppose the Attorney General knows his business too well to denominate any offence a libel, and to prosecute it by information only, if he means to have it considered as high treason.

Indeed, I have heard in discourse, that a certain laborious minister has whispered many of his friends, "whatever they "might hear from others, that the law-officers of the crown "had assured him, Mr. Wilkes might have been prosecuted "for high treason; but however, they were not willing "to push things against him to the utmost." An assertion that is scarcely to be parallelled (I believe) for its folly, profligacy or effrontery; and which, in a country where nothing can be done but by law, deserves no other answer than this, "I wish you had attempted it, for, if you had, it would have ruined you, and you would have deserved "it, as the only adequate reward for your pains." The Epping-forest case would not warrant this position, I can assure him; and I am certain he has a private friend, a candid lawyer, who would strongly dissuade him from really making so ridiculous an attempt. I say this, because I suppose the minister himself, is now become so Right Honourable, that he ceases any longer to be learned in the laws of his country.

" The E. of Bristol, having exhibited a charge of Trea-
" son against the E. of Clarendon, alledged, That he had
" endeavoured to alienate the affections of his Majesty's

G " subjects,

" subjects, by venting *opprobious scandals* against his Ma-
" jesty's *person*, and that he had traduced *both houses of*
" *parliament*. The Judges were ordered to give their
" opinion whether this be any treason or no? They unani-
" mously agreed, That if the matters alleged in the charge
" were admitted to be true, altho' alleged to be *traito-*
" *rously done*, yet there is no Treason in it."

Why then, is the Attorney angry with any other man for talking of No. 45, as a libel? He himself, with all his elaborate perplexity of language, can tell no more? Why need he search for words to denominate " seditious " writings, a subtle poison, the feed of jealousy, revolt " and discord, the parent at least, if not the offspring, " of treason?" (Or why not both parent and offspring at one and the same time: the sense will not be hurt, and the creed be more orthodox?) In every light he can put these writings, they will appear the same, their nature will not alter, they will still be but libels.

Indeed there is a great deal of difference between libel and libel, as between other individuals of one and the same species, some having more and others less wit, some being more and others less personal, some levelled against the establishment, and others against that varying thing a ministry. For example, *The Sixth Letter to the People of England* was a most gross attack upon the present constitution and succession; but *The Test, the Letter versified,* and *Rodondo*, were merely personal abuse upon Mr. Pitt, his Lady, and her eldest Brother. *Mock-Patriotism* took a middle flight between the abuse of one or two individuals, and that of a whole party; altho' for the beauty of its images, the happiness of its allusions, and the elegance of its expressions, it was *rara avis* in this predicament of writers: none of whom however were without some wit and merit; excepting always, the dull and rancorous Jacobite first named. In truth, abusive satire has been dealt in pretty equally of all sides, and the only measure has been the abilities of the respective penmen. When somebody shewed a North Briton to old Johnson, turning his definition of a pensioner upon himself, he very cleverly answered, " It " is fair enough, I have no reason to complain.

" *Nec lex justior ulla*
" *Quam necis artifices arte perire sua.*"

After

After all, the Attorney himself cannot help speaking of the composition of libels as an exercise of wit, and thereupon " supposing the author of *The Budget* may chuse by " and bye to *amuse* himself this very way;" and then roundly charges this gentleman " with personal indecency " and his" supposed " friend with acrimony, envy, spleen, " conceitedness and self-importance" as mere flowers, I presume, of rhetorick, well becoming the pen of a ministerial writer against libels. And, he speaks of the ruin of a virtuous patriot by an information, with as much glee, as an old letcher does of the debauching of a comely virgin by ravishment.

Nobody without doors thinks the case of any " libel justifies strongly," or at all, " the practice of general warrants," if it were only for this reason, that every party against whom a libel is levelled, always christens it seditious, treasonable and what not; and yet, whether it be any libel at all, no man has a right to pronounce, before a Jury of the country has determined it to be one. They are likewise less necessary in this than any other offence, because the publisher must always be known and may be come at, whether the author be so or not. And " it would " be (as Hawkins says) extremely hard, to leave it to the " discretion of a common officer to arrest what persons, and " search what houses he thinks fit: and if a Justice cannot " legally grant a blank warrant for the arrest of a single " person, leaving it to the party to fill it up, surely he cannot " grant such a general warrant, which might have the " effect of an hundred blank warrants."

With respect to the warrant of Lord H. if the form had really been according to the " uninterrupted practice " of the Secretary of State's office." This would not have made it legal. But even this is not a fact; for one cannot help remarking, that the old Tories under Queen Anne, the Revolution still tingling in their ears, were exceedingly cautious, consulting council, probably upon the warrant itself, before they ventured to take up a subject; insomuch, that all the warrants even of Lord Bolingbroke, whilst he was Secretary of State, appear to be strictly legal. In truth, there has been no uniform practice in the office, as may be seen by the variant and multiform warrants printed from thence in *Quarto*, and privately distributed to trusty friends by P. C. W. with the inscription of *most secret*. Much less would precedents only from the time of the Revolution be sufficient to *justify* such an illegal practice. And as to the pretence that this practice " did " not then take its rise, having been frequent in former " reigns, reaching back *perhaps* to the remotest times, and " combined with the very essence of government," it is totally groundless; for, after the most diligent search, no warrants of a similar form could be found higher than the reign of the Stuarts, but few of them, and of those few hardly more than one of an antienter date than Bennet Lord Arlington, Secretary to Charles the 2d. From such premises, however, this hardened writer would insinuate, that perhaps they were used in the remotest times, and are of the essence of government. This notable antiquity of office is indeed further supported by a note, which takes notice that the act of Henry the 8th, settling precedency, mentions, among other officers, the King's Secretary. It does so. And what of that? This was the æra of the reformation of Religion; but, I never heard before it was the commencement of civil government. No prior mention, however, of King's Secretaries, as officers of State, could I suppose be found, and therefore this or none must be cited. Is this now, in the name of common sense, a proof of immemorial existence? The fact is, in antient times, the King had only a private Secretary for his Privy Council; there was no such person as a Secretary of State. He is the production of times within memory (to speak as a lawyer;) and none of the many books which treat of the great officers of State, and the *Aula Regis*, make any mention of such a Being. The 2d of Richard II, which gives the action of *Scandalum magnatum*, in the enumeration of great officers of State, does not notice either the King's Secretary or the members of his Privy Council. There is no mention made by *Fortescue*, Lord Chancellor to Henry the 6th, in a book on *absolute and limited Government*, which he wrote under the reign of Edward the 4th, where he considers the King's Council and the great officers about the throne, of the Secretary. In truth, the Secretary's consequence and power arose from his being admitted a member of the Privy Council, and as such alone it is that he can pretend to the power of commitment. This does not make him, however, a Justice of Peace, and

more

more authority he never claimed. To render him so, it has of late been always the practice to insert by name every Privy Counsellor into the commissions of the peace, that from time to time pass for the several counties. So that the two grounds suggested as an authority for the issuing of these General Warrants, namely, the constant exercise and usage of them, and the antiquity of the Secretary of State as a Privy Counsellor, both fail. But, had they both been good, they would not have authorized these warrants; because, a practice of the like sort, must be supported by uniform usage; and the warrants produced, differed so much in their form, that hardly any three of them were exactly alike. The greatest part too of the warrants offered in proof of this custom and pretended right, were issued in the times of rebellion; when men are not likely to call in question such a proceeding, the extremity of the case making them wink at all irregularities, for the sake of supporting the protestant establishment itself. And yet, bad men, as one may easily figure to one self, will be apt to lay stress upon such acts of necessity, as precedents for their doing the like in ordinary cases, and to gratify personal pique, and therefore such excesses of power are dangerous in example, and should never be excused, but when it appears that government could not be defended or upheld without actual recourse to them. But, even if the usage had been both immemorial and uniform, and ten thousand similar warrants could have been produced, it would not have been sufficient; because, the practice must likewise be agreeable to the principles of law, in order to be good, whereas, this is a practice inconsistent with, and in direct opposition to, the first and clearest principles of law. Immemorial uniform usage will not even support the bye-law of a corporation, if it be flatly repugnant to the fundamentals of the common law; much less, will it authorise the secret practice of a political office. In one word, no warrant whatever, in any case or crime whatever, that names or describes nobody in certain, is good, or can be justified in law, in any circumstances whatever. Therefore, if that point alone had been put in question, I do not see how any " thinking " and honest man could have fairly voted against it." The law is too well established to be rendered doubtful, by all the dexterity of the Attorney or his Coadjutor.

Eight

Eight years of ingenious judicature will scarcely accomplish so arduous a task.

The Attorney might as well say, that Lord H. when using the power of a Justice of the Peace by virtue of his office of Secretary of State, could make an illegal warrant as a Magistrate, good as a military officer, by styling himself *Lieutenant General of his Majesty's Forces*, and commanding all *military officers to assist as there shall be occasion*. The circumstance, tho' new, I am seriously of opinion, is as good an argument in law, as what can be derived from the usage of a Secretary of State's office.

Moreover, it is not true, even in a political sense, that a declaration of the illegality of all General Warrants whatever, would " take away from the executive power, an " authority which may be frequently found essential to " the very being of the State." For, if in case of High Treason (the only crime that need ever occasion a stretch of authority, and even That very rarely) there should be a necessity for the apprehension of people, whose names, or any certain designation of their persons, could not be had, and this was made afterwards to appear; as That is a crime which tends to the dissolution of the whole frame of government, there is no doubt but the minister would be excused for the dictatorial power he should exercise, *pro salute Reipublicæ*, upon such an emergency. But I would have such things as emergent necessities applied to his pardon, and not to his justification.

Therefore, I see no reason why a man should not vote for the condemnation of General Warrants in all cases, without limiting his damnation to General Warrants in the case of seditious libels. " The propositions are different," but in the eye of the law, these General Warrants are in both cases equally illegal. In short, if this was not the constitution, I think " we might amuse the public with the sound of liberty," but should really enjoy none. If such warrants were to be allowed legally justifiable in any instances, it would be exceedingly difficult, nay, impossible, to restrain Ministers from grievously oppressing any man they did not like, under many pretences, from time to time, for their own safety, without any motive of public good. I agree, therefore, with the Attorney, in saying, that " if the liberty of the subject be the great
" object.

" object in view, and be incompatible with General
" Warrants in one instance, it is inconsistent with the
" same warrants in any other. There is no exception to
" be made to our *general* reasoning." The grievance extends to all persons, of all degrees, of all qualities; it is *commune periculum*.

As to the suggestion that experience has proved " there
" is only a possibility of danger to the liberty of the sub-
" ject, from the exercise of this power;" it is a most slippery argument, and of no real weight whatever.

For, in the first place, these warrants have been rarely exercised, until of late years, and perhaps never before, in the case of a libel, upon one of the Representatives of the people. Every thing of this sort is practised with some tenderness at first. Tyranny grows by degrees. Besides, few common men have private purses sufficient to contend with That of the Public and the power of the crown, both of which are used by every Minister, to the utmost extent, upon such occasions. Sometimes too, the private prosecutor is bought off.

In the next place, if the experience of these warrants had been so great, and no mischief to the subject had hitherto ensued; yet, who, in a very momentous concern, no less than the liberty of every man in England, would let even a possibility of abuse remain, that was able to get rid of it. It is not within the power of any legislature, to prevent every private man or minister from committing abuses by an infraction of the law; but, I think, no wise legislature would give such a sanction to any bad or arbitrary usage, as would afford a *handle* to all ministers to be guilty of the greatest abuses, impunedly, and under the colour of law.

Upon a supposition that the foregoing arguments will not do, the Attorney closes his ratiocination on this point, with saying, that " the Court of King's Bench had ad-
" mitted persons to bail, apprehended under such war-
" rants, instead of giving them their full discharge, and
" that this circumstance is of so much importance to the
" question, of the legality of the warrants, that in the
" opinion of an old experienced and able Lawyer upon
" the occasion, who will ever be esteemed an honour to
" his profession, it implies no less than an imputation of
" perjury, to suppose such practise to have prevailed in
" the

" the Court of King's Bench, unless the legality of the warrants had been at the same time acknowledged by that Court." Now, who this old Lawyer is, I don't know, nor the date of the friendship between him and the Attorney. But, if I were to guess, it must be some antiquated Tory, who till lately was as uniformly against, as he now is uniformly for, all measures, and who only comes out upon extraordinary occasions, with a grave face, to do extraordinary work. One of your staunch men, that goes plump through thick and thin, and to advance such doctrine, must, I think, have gone through the thickest of it, and consequently appear in a very dirty light to all other Lawyers upon his emerging. I dare say, 20 years ago, the same man would have vouched as strongly to the cure of the King's Evil by the touch of the true royal line. In my conscience, he could find no one Lawyer besides to countenance him in such doctrine; or, if he did, it must be some old gentleman of the same Tory kidney. Now, the Tory-principles are such, that I should have been much better satisfied of the truth of this dogma, had the Attorney himself directly affirmed, upon the credit of his own character as a Lawyer, that an admission to bail under a General Warrant, proves either the warrant to be legal, or the Judge to be perjured. But, it is very singular that the Attorney will not affirm any thing of himself in this matter, any more than he did upon the article of usage, but chuses to slip in the assertion of some antient invalid, or *miles emeritus*, for the purpose, whom he puts in the front of the battle; and then, if he can but pick up some other superannuating stager, of the like original concoction, he will, of the two, form a most excellent forlorn hope. By the bye, if any veteran Black Letter could be brought up to such an affirmation, in a grave and serious manner, as *amicus curiæ*, I should think, under any other than the present Whig administration, his merit would be so transcendent, that he might expect the Minister's interest for a peerage for himself, or otherwise for his son, as he should like best. At this time, however, I should imagine, he would only find he had absolutely thrown away his character to no purpose at all. Old Hunters say, there is nothing like trying a man at once at a six bar gate; for, if he ventures to

take

take that, you may be sure of his going over every thing else with ease.

After all, let me ask, Does the Court of *King's Bench*, or any other court, when a man is brought before them, examine into the warrant, unless the person apprehended makes an objection thereto? Nay, is not the very contrary every day's experience? Is it not even the desire of the party taken up, nine times in ten, to be bailed; as he knows, upon his discharge from that arrest, another warrant in a regular form would be immediately issued? Would it be right therefore in a Judge to scrutinize the validity of every *capias*? In truth, bailing is a matter of course, where no objection is taken, and there is no pretence for saying this act of course is an acknowlegement by the Court of the validity of the warrant, or of the regularity of the arrest. Every apprehension is supposed to be legally made. A man might as well suggest, that the Chancellor reads every writ he signs, before it is issued, to see whether it be clerically drawn; or that a Judge never tries a cause at *nisi prius*, until he has examined the whole of the process, and seen all to be regular. Now, I will venture to affirm that Judges never examine the process at all, unless one of the parties move the Court specially for the purpose. *Consensus tollit errorem.* And, no man ever suggested that they broke their oaths by not doing this *ex officio*; indeed, if the extravagant doctrine here advanced were true, not one of the present reverend bench could now be free from perjury. In short, such a speech, if it were made, is a proof of nothing, but the shameless length to which party is capable of carrying a Tory: for, no lawyer ever practised in a court of law, especially at the head of a great circuit, that did not in his own practice, meet with a multitude of instances, which flatly contradict this violent position. Every common lawyer of a year's standing can vouch the contrary. Nay, were it not so, the Attorney knows it to be a maxim among lawyers, that " what is done without de-
" bate, or any argument or consideration had of it, makes
" the authority of a precedent to be of no force in point
" of law: for, judgments and awards, given upon delibe-
" ration and debate, only are proofs and arguments of
" weight; and not any sudden act of the court without
" debate or deliberation.

The Attorney sees nothing alarming in the seizure of a Member's papers and bureaus upon the charge of a libel only, and reproaches a late writer with "-heightening the "the picture upon this occasion, by the introduction of "sacks and messengers." Now, I understand nothing is mentioned by this writer, that was not an undoubted fact, and, if I know the Attorney aright, he likes to debate upon a fact, and for that reason would throw every circumstance into a case, however unnecessary this may seem to many people, who think it best always to argue and determine upon the general principle. Provided then the fact be so, I can frame to myself, no circumstance capable of adding to the terror of such a scene, whilst laws exist, unless it be the representation of the whole as transacted, and by particular order, at midnight. I chuse, however, not to dwell upon this lawless part of the story, and, as my son in his letter hath said a good deal about the absolute illegality of the seizure of papers, I shall here say very little more concerning this abominable outrage; altho', I think it, to use the words of Mr. Somers, " the worst means to arrive at the worst ends "imaginable."

According to my notions, no words can convey to the mind of the reader, the anxiety which a man may feel from such a distress. Many gentlemen have secret correspondences, which they keep from their wives, their relations, and their bosom friends. Every body has some private papers, that he would not on any account have revealed. A lawyer hath frequently the papers and securities of his clients; a merchant or agent, of his correspondents. What then, can be more excruciating torture, than to have the lowest of mankind, such fellows as Mooney, Watson, and the rest of them, enter suddenly into his house, and forcibly carry away his scrutores, with all his papers of every kind, under a pretence of law, *because* the Attorney general had, *ex officio*, filed an information against the author, printer and publisher of some pamphlet or weekly paper, and somebody had told one of these greyhounds that this gentleman was thought by some people to be the author! These papers are immediately to be thrown into the hands of some clerks, of much curiosity, and of very little business in times of peace, who will, upon being bid to sort and select those that relate to

such

such and such a particular thing, naturally amuse themselves with the perusal of all private letters, memorandums, secrets and intrigues, of the gentleman himself, and of all his friends and acquaintance of both sexes. In the hurry too of such a business, notes, bonds, or even deeds, and evidence of the utmost consequence to private property, may be divulged, lost, torn or destroyed, to his irreparable injury.

I will now, for a moment, suppose that this gentleman had actually wrote, in the hours of his wantonness or folly, something that was really abusive and scandalous upon some particular minister, or upon the administration in general. Even in such a case, would any gentleman in this kingdom rest one minute at ease in his bed, if he thought, that for every loose and unguarded, or supposed libellous expression, about party-matters, he was liable not only to be taken up himself, but every secret of his family made subject to the inspection of a whole Secretary of State's Office, or indeed, of any man or minister whatever, whilst a parliament was sitting, or had even an existence in the country.

Such a vexatious authority in the crown, is inconsistent with every idea of liberty. It seems to me to be the highest of libels upon the constitution, to pretend, that any usage can justify such an act of arbitrary government. The laws of England, are so tender to every man accused, even of capital crimes, that they do not permit him to be put to torture to extort a confession, nor oblige him to answer a question that will tend to accuse himself. How then can it be supposed, that the Law will intrust any officer of the crown, with the power of charging any man in the Kingdom (or, indeed, every man by possibility and nobody in particular) at his will and pleasure, with being the author, printer or publisher of such a paper, being a libel, and which till a jury has determined to be so, is nothing; and that upon this *charge*, any common fellows under a general warrant, upon their own imaginations, or the surmises of their acquaintance, or upon other worse and more dangerous intimations, may, with a strong hand, seize and carry off all his papers; and then at his trial produce these papers, thus taken by force from him, in evidence against himself; and all this on the charge of a mere misdemeanor, in a country of liberty and property. This would

would be making a man give evidence againſt and accuſe himſelf, with a vengeance. And this is to be endured, becauſe the proſecutor wants other ſufficient proof, and might be traduced for acting groundleſly, if he could not get it; and becauſe he does it truly for the ſake of *collecting evidence*.

I ſhould not have given myſelf the trouble of ſaying thus much in ſo plain a matter, had it not been for a letter which was printed ſome time ago, upon this ſubject, with the names of two noble lords, ſecretaries of ſtate, ſubſcribed. It is directed "to Mr. Wilkes," dated "Great George-ſtreet, May the 7th, 1763," and contains the following expreſſions:

"SIR,

"In anſwer to your letter of yeſterday, we acquaint you, that your papers were ſeized in conſequence of the heavy charge brought againſt you, for being the author of an infamous and ſeditious libel, for which, notwithſtanding your diſcharge from your commitment to the Tower, His Majeſty has ordered you to be proſecuted; by his Attorney-general. Such of your papers as do not lead to a proof of your guilt, ſhall be reſtored to you: Such as are neceſſary for that purpoſe, it was our duty to deliver over to thoſe, whoſe office it is to *collect the evidence*, and manage the proſecution againſt you. We are

"Your humble Servants,

" Egremont.
" Dunk Halifax."

Here now is a clear avowal of the principle of taking theſe papers. The evidence indeed, ſeems to have been *collected* with as much force, and I believe with as little right by law, as ſome other collections are made for which the collectors are hanged when taken. I cannot but ſay, therefore, I am very glad this letter has been publiſhed, that the Public may ſee what is the notion of law in thoſe political offices, that are now attempting to prove their lawleſs practices to be the ancient common law of the Land.

One

One Instance of the legislature's regard to the privacy of papers and correspondence, may be seen in the act regulating the post-office, whereby, every post-master and clerk, is forbid to *open* any letter, upon any pretence whatever, except, by warrant of one of the principal Secretaries of State; who, if the mere opening should afterwards be questioned, is thereby rendered under his hand responsible for the same.

When the D. of Newcastle was minister, under a general sweeping warrant, the messengers seized some copper-plates of the late Rebels' victories, whereupon the owner commenced an action; shortly after which Mr. P. his attorney, was called upon by a certain noted solicitor, who told him, that the Government would not return the plates, but would, however, make satisfaction for them. Mr. P. said, that he would not dissuade his client from making up the matter, but, that as the seizure was wholly unwarrantable, he must be handsomely repaired in damages, and therefore he would not advise him to take less than 200l. upon such an occasion. The noted Solicitor agreed to, and paid the sum demanded, upon having a release of the action; altho' it was very clear, the real injury did not amount to 50l. Thus dropped and expired this action, as has been the case with many others before and since. In short, one way or other, the proceedings in these matters never come before the Public. The Parties are either too indigent to contend with the Crown, or else the Crown buys them off. Attornies too, for the most part, are afraid both of incensing men in power and of losing their costs, by being concerned for poor and obnoxious clients, who may either run away, or be tampered with by the Solicitor for the Treasury. For which reasons, it is extremely difficult to cite adjudged cases, in such very clear points: and, therefore, one must decide upon them by general maxims and principles of common law, which are, indeed, a much more unerring guide than any particular case, of which it is ten to one whether you can obtain any correct and authentic report.

If such a power of seizing papers could be supported by law, is it to be imagined, that no declaration of it should have been made from the Bench, by the several able and learned Chief Justices of England, who have presided in the King's Courts since this practice has taken place.

place. Many of them have been warm friends of administration, and they could not have rendered a minister so formidable, especially in times of violent party and disaffection, by any other means whatever. Nay, some of them have had opportunities of making this declaration, and yet have studiously avoided it, for which no reason can be assigned, but their knowing the practice to be illegal. A stronger, negative argument can hardly be produced.

Nothing, as I apprehend, can be forcibly taken from any man, or his house entered, without some specific charge upon oath. The mansion of every man being his castle, no general search-warrant is good. It must either be sworn that I have certain stolen goods, or such a particular thing that is criminal in itself, in my custody, before any magistrate is authorised to grant a warrant to any man to enter my house and seize it. Nay further, if a positive oath be made, and such a particular warrant be issued, it can only be executed upon the paper or thing sworn to and specified, and in the presence of the owner, or of somebody intrusted by him, with the custody of it. Without these limitations, there is no liberty or free enjoyment of person or property, but every part of a man's most valuable possessions and privacies, is liable to the ravage, inroad and inspection of suspicious ministers, who may at any time harrass, insult and expose, and perhaps, undo him. Nay, whenever they suspect there is evidence against themselves, they may, by this boundless authority, seize and carry it away, in order to defeat prosecution.

In misdemeanor, felony or treason, before conviction, the personal property of the accused, remains unaltered; no magistrate has a right to examine the whole, nor to touch or seize any particular part, without some special information on oath as to individual things. And upon what legal foundation, a contrary practice has been set afoot, I am totally at a loss to guess.

L. C. J. Hale lays down these rules, as to warrants to search for stolen goods, " (1.) They are not to be grant-
" ed without oath, made before a Justice, of a felony
" committed, and that the party complaining has pro-
" bable cause to suspect they are in such a house or
" place, and do shew his reasons for his suspicion; and
" there-

" therefore a general warrant to search all suspected
" places is not good; nor are general warrants dormant,
" justifiable, nor do they give any more power to the
" officer or party, than what he had without them.
" (2.) It is fit to express that search be made in the day-
" time. (3.) They should be directed to constables and
" not to private persons, tho' the person complaining
" should be present, because he knows his goods. (4.) It
" ought to command that the goods found, together with
" the party in whose custody they are found, be brought
" before some Justice of the peace."

The first warrant that ever was granted for seizing papers generally, was, by Lord Townshend, in the reign of George the first; until that time, no secretary of state ever went farther than to direct the seizure of some papers particularized.

In such a party-crime, as a public libel, who can endure this assumed authority of taking all papers indiscriminately? When, in such a crime as forgery, or any other felony; or even in that dangerous crime, high treason, by correspondence with traitors or the king's enemies, all men would cry out against it, and most deservedly! Nothing can be touched, without some criminal charge in law specifically sworn against it. And where there is even a charge against one particular paper, to seize *all*, of every kind, is extravagant, unreasonable and inquisitorial. It is infamous in theory, and downright tyranny and despotism in practice. We can have no positive liberty or privacy, but must enjoy our correspondencies, friendships, papers and studies at discretion, that is, at the will and pleasure of the ministers for the time being, and of their inferior agents!

Had Charles the second thought his ministers intitled to this prerogative, he would not have resorted to parliament for sweeping warrants, to search for and seize all seditious and treasonable books and pamphlets. His messenger of the press would have ranged through the shops of booksellers and printers, and the studies of disaffected persons, that is, of sticklers for liberty, upon the mere warrant of a Secretary of State or privy counsellor, without the aid of a licensing statute.

And let me here ask a question. If a libel be no actual breach of the peace, and sureties for the peace or the

be-

behaviour be not demandable of the supposed libeller; by what colour of law, or by what warrant or capias, can any man, charged as the writer or publisher, have his doors and locks broken open, for the apprehension either of himself or his papers? Can such force be authorised by virtue of any legal process whatever, in this species of misdemeanor, before verdict, nay before judgment?*

Nevertheless, I have heard, that a candid lawyer has lately engaged for the seizure of papers, declaring " no government can stand without such power." But the speech or the scripture of a trimming man, is not, I hope, to be counted for gospel. And, I am clear, that many glorious governments have stood without it, and that no administration or government ought to stand, that wants it. However, it is easy to foretel that so flattering a subscriber to any political tenets, cannot long himself withstand any thing. He would be able, I should think, if occasion presented, to throw himself at the feet of any Majesty, with as much affection and ardency, as the most

---

* In a printed account of the transaction of Mr. Wilkes' case, it is stated thus : " *The 26th of April,* a general Warrant was issued against the Authors, Printers and Publishers of N°. 45, and 49 Persons were apprehended by it before the 29th, and among them a reputable tradesman. This last was taken out of bed from his wife and a child dangerously ill, his house disordered and his papers ransacked, and his person detained three days after his innocence known. *The 29th,* the Secretaries of State received complete information that Mr. Wilkes was the author and publisher; and, the general warrant still remaining in the messengers hands, by virtue thereof, on *the 30th,* Mr. Wilkes's house was forcibly entered, his doors and locks broken open, all his papers thrown into a sack and committed to the hands of common messengers, without any schedule or security for the return of them. Mr. Wilkes himself was carried before Lord H. where it was immediately made known, that an *Habeas Corpus* was applied for and expected every moment, but, to avoid the effect of that writ, he was hurried away to the Tower, and there all access was denied to him, as well as the use of pen, ink and paper." And I will add, from my own knowledge, that those who had the searching of his papers divulged the contents of some private letters, which might have been very prejudicial to the writer of them, and have hurt his interest and his friendship with other friends.

"It has been asserted that, in search of Monsieur D'Eon, found a libeller by a Jury, in order to take and bring him into the King's Bench to receive judgment on the verdict, the doors and locks of chambers, closets and scrutores, were broke open; altho' it was denied he was there, and it afterwards appeared he was not there. This was said to be done by virtue of a Capias from the K. B. by some, and by others of a Secretary of State's warrant, but without any information upon oath of his being in such house; and merely upon a slight suspicion, that he might be there, grounded upon his having been seen about two months before going to the house.

pro-

proftrate or adulatory of *Hague*-minifters. An outward decency and deliberation, in every ftep, will enable a man, at laft, to ferve the more effectually, and even to impofe a wrong fenfe upon the old revolution motto of *Prodeſſe quam conſpici*. And yet there is, after all, fuch a thing as outwitting one'sfelf, and being the dupe of one's own cunning, after having made this left-handed wifdom the ftudy of one's life, from the tendereft infancy.

The Attorney having flightly paffed over the feizure of papers, after talking of it as a mere picture for which he happened to have no tafte, *intirely* omits the fubfequent grievance of the *cloſe* confinement; and, my fon, having fomewhat touched that matter in his letter, I fhall not expatiate upon the fubject, fo much, at leaft, as the importance of it would otherwife have inclined me to. Any body, however, who looks at the warrant of commitment, will fee the direction to the conftable of the Tower, is not merely to keep Mr. Wilkes fafe, but " to keep him " fafe and *cloſe*, until he fhall be delivered by due courfe " of law." Now, the cuftody here directed, is unwarrantable in law, in the cafe of a mifdemeanor, nay in any cafe.

The common commitments ufed by Juftices of the peace, even in cafes of robbery on the highway, and other felonies, not entitled to clergy, are *to receive into your goal, and him ſafely to keep*, or *that you ſafely keep*, or *there to remain (until delivered by law)*; *ſalvo cuſtodiri, ad ſalvo cuſtodiendum, ſalvo cuſtodias, in ſalva cuſtodia ut detineatur*, or at moft *ſalvo & ſecure cuſtodiri*: infomuch, that out of all the various forms of mittimus's to be met with in *Burn's Juſtice*, or the *Regiſtrum Brevium*, there is not one where the word *cloſe* or *arcta*, is inferted.

When a goaler is to keep his prifoner fafe, he is only to reftrain him fo as to prevent his efcape, and no perfon not dangerous, in that refpect, is to be hindered from having accefs to him, in the day-time. But, when the order is to keep the prifoner fafe and *cloſe*, the goaler is to fhut him up from all the world. By a printed paper too, handed about, I learn that the warders of the Tower, in this laft cafe, are never to leave their prifoner one moment alone. And, in a paper which Mr. Wilkes difperfed, he afferted that thefe orders were ftrictly obferved with refpect to him, infomuch, that altho' he was com-

I mitted

mitted Satururday the 30th of April, yet it was Tuesday May the 3d, after having been brought up by Habeas Corpus to the Court of Common Pleas, and remanded, before his friends, had for the first time, free access to him. His Council and Attorney had made repeated applications for admission on Saturday, Sunday and Monday, as well as his brother, a noble Earl, and several people of distinction; and on the Monday, he happened to see himself a written order upon Major Ransford's table, directing him even to take down the names of all persons applying for admittance. The common report about town was, that the secretary of state went to his country-house on the Saturday morning, and did not return till Tuesday noon, and therefore no order for the admission of any person could be had, and that the Major would not break through his general orders about *close* prisoners at the desire of the solicitor of the treasury: but, this could never be the reason, as it was very easy to have sent a messenger 10 or 12 miles out of town, to the secretary's villa, when the prisoner was a Member of Parliament, and the public begun to be alarmed.

I am more inclined to believe another report, namely, that the Major received particular, positive, verbal orders at first, to let nobody have access to him, and that he declared, had it not been for Those, he should not have scrupled to have let in any of Mr. Wilkes's friends or relations, notwithstanding the word *close* was inserted in the warrant. In short, it was a misconception of the lawful power. The great civil officers imagined there was no difference at all made by the law between the treatment of a prisoner committed for a misdemeanor, and of one for a capital crime, or before or after conviction.

Now, my opinion is, that before conviction the law does not warrant close confinement, so as to debar a friend from access, in any case whatever; and that the same is a breach of the great *Habeas Corpus* law, and of all the statutes *de Homine replegiando*. For, if a man when apprehended and carried before a magistrate, is, by that magistrate committed forthwith to close custody, so that nobody can get at him, it will be impossible for him to write a letter, or to make an affidavit, to get a Habeas Corpus. Indeed, it seems to me to be an absolute deprivation of the right that every subject has to his liberty, " unless it shall appear that the party so committed, is
" de-

" detained upon a legal procefs, order or warrant, out
" of fome court that has a jurifdiction of criminal mat-
" ters, or by fome warrant of fome Judge or Juftice of
" Peace for fuch matter or offence for which by law the
" prifoner is not bailable." This ftatute of Charles the
2d, takes notice of the " great delays and other *Shifts*
" of goalers and *others*, contrary to the known laws,
" whereby many of the King's fubjects, may be long
" detained in prifon, in fuch cafes, where by law they
" are bailable, to their great charges and vexation," and
purports to be exprefly enacted, " for the prevention
" thereof, and the more fpeedy relief of all perfons im-
" prifoned for any criminal or fuppofed criminal matters."
Now, if I do not mifremember, the five members were
committed to *clofe* confinement, for feditious difcourfes in
parliament, by Charles the 1ft, and it was the agitation of
this very queftion that firft fhook his throne ; and yet, I do
not know, that in the cafe of Mr. Wilkes, it has ever been
taken notice of at all, either in parliament or in any court
of Juftice.

I look upon clofe cuftody in fuch an offence as a libel,
the leaft definable and the moft ambiguous of all mifde-
meanors, and by conftruction only a breach of the peace,
to be not only abfolutely illegal, but extreme cruelty in
itfelf, and, with refpect to the conftitution, the moft law-
lefs tyranny that can be exerted by any minifter, and fuch
as ought to make every gentleman ftartle, when he thinks
of it only.

It is not the corporal injury that conftitutes, in the eyes
of mankind, the dreadfulnefs of the example. It is the
force exerted and continued againft law.

When I fee a fecretary of ftate, obftinately fighting
with the laws of his country, ufing privilege to the utmoft,
notwithftanding it was the ground of the royal complaint
to the Commons againft Mr. Wilkes, availing himfelf of
every practicable effoign, and, at length, withftanding
all the procefs and penalties of a court of Juftice, to a-
void trying the right of a tranfaction, which has never
yet been directly given up ; and perhaps waiting for an
outlawry of his profecutor, in order then to mock the
juftice of his country ftill more, by entering an appearance to the fuit againft him, at a time, when his profecutor can no longer go on with it : I proteft, altho' an

old,

old, sober, private individual, that I lose my temper, look for redress from some other quarter, and feel myself inclined to join in an address to the Commons of England, to take up the consideration, and go on with the prosecution of that cause, which every Freeman is interested in, and which the ordinary courts of justice have been so long foiled in. I remember what is Mr. Locke's definition of liberty; what he makes the province of a court of judicature; what the extent of the legislative power; and what, according to him, creates a dissolution of all government.

Who under such circumstances would blame a Jury, should they at last have such a secretary brought before them, for giving extraordinary, exemplary damages, *in terrorem?* Especially, if they should have all imaginable foundation for believing the judgment upon such verdict, will be delayed by every artifice of bills of exceptions, special verdicts, motions for new trial, writs of error, &c. that can be practised, in order to prevent all effect from it, and to overbear, in the long run, the poor prosecutor by dint of expence.

If mankind is to be enraged, I really think this is the readiest way to effect it.

If a questionable act has been done by the great officers of a state in any just government, and when taken notice of, they avoid a decision of the established courts of law, I will say they disserve the Crown by such conduct, let who will advise it. It is unbecoming men who pretend to an honourable repute or a justifiable behaviour, and incredible where an administration means only to use legal powers or desires to know what they are.

No jury will give great damages where a minister pleads law for his excuse, and readily resorts to a court of law for its opinion, in order to shew the truth of his plea. But where he shuffles and cuts, flies to privilege and chicane, and avoids a court of law, or keeps it at bay, he will not only have every presumption in disfavour of him, but will raise the resentment of every man, and should the slow foot of justice at last overtake him, nobody will think it can treat him too severely, as an example to all future ministers.

How can any minister think of eluding the laws, when he considers that kings, the supreme magistrates of this country,

country, hold their crown by no other tenure, and are sworn and bound to govern by law, at the peril of that very crown itself! Our constitution admits of no arbitrary will or pleasure in any man. The law is the sole sovereign of England, and That law is known and settled, on the firm basis of immemorable usage, innumerable precedents through a succession of ages, and upon the statutes of kings, lords, and commons. And, it is this circumstance which makes the security, the independence, and the pre-eminent felicity of Englishmen. What a comfort is it to every man, who either raises or inherits a fortune, to hold That and his liberty by the same and as good a title as his King holds his crown? Who therefore, can sink so low as to submit to enjoy, all that he has, by the mere grace and favour of a man like himself, instead of holding it independent of every thing upon earth, but the known and necessary laws of society.

It would, in my poor opinion, be of infinite use to young men of fortune, beginning the great world, who may hereafter be ministers of state, to read attentively the first 15 years of the reign of Charles the I. and the last 16 years before the Revolution, in the original diaries, annals, memoirs, tracts, and in the parliamentary and cotemporary histories, of those days. They would thereby perceive, what mighty ill consequences flow from small beginnings, and particularly, from right not being to be had for the subject in courts of Justice.

The Attorney wonders, what should occasion any "alarm" and says, one would think, " that some inno-" cent man had been oppressed by arbitrary violence, " tyranny, and persecution." To which I shall only say, that the legality of the arrest itself by virtue of such a warrant, and not the innocence of the man arrested, is the matter in question.

The Attorney might as well talk of the qualities of the writer's mind, and endeavour to shew that he was a ludicrous, extravagant, profligate, debauched and blasphemous fellow, and wrote an infamous poem, whereby he excited the indignation of a grave and pious nobleman, who, from a motive of conscience complained of him to the house of lords, for disporting himself in the works of Vice; and that therefore, such a man might be treated as administration should please, without any regard to law or the constitution,

stitution, and that, instead of protecting the franchises of their countrymen, the parliament should only settle the morals of individuals, like the Courts Christian of Bishops.

The Attorney concludes on this head with asking, whether all the printers and other " parties aggrieved, deny " that they have had ample satisfaction?" whereby he indirectly admits that they had been *aggrieved*, but then insinuates, that as money is in his mind the measure of all things, and an adequate consideration either for a broken head or a broken constitution, so there has been no harm done at all, but what is now compleatly paid for. Let me ask, were these damages offered or even paid voluntarily, so soon as the unlawfulness of the act was discovered? Or, were they extorted, by the verdict of a jury; after every means to delay and to defeat the action, to stagger the Judge who tried the cause (but who was too firm to be frightened, and too able to be imposed upon) and finally, to suspend indefinitely the judgment upon this verdict, by a bill of exceptions, had been tried in vain? After all this, were the exceptions tendered with such earnestness, and so much appearance of sincerity, ever argued or deemed capable of support in any court of law whatever? Or, were the persons, who took them, after these fruitless attempts to delude mankind, under the sacred names of law and constitution, obliged, like convicted jugglers, to give up the game, and, as the last shift, to buy off clandestinely the verdicts so publickly obtained, in hopes, by a private barter of satisfaction and release from low and ignorant prosecutors, to nick an attorney, who had laboured a just and a national suit, out of his costs? Is this, or is it not the Truth; and is or is it not a handsome come off, or a reputable way of giving up a great cause, where the Crown has thought proper by its Attorney General to take up the defence? *Sume superbiam quæsitam meritis.*

But in God's name, what have damages to do with the great point the Attorney is arguing, whether the Commons of England should or should not come to a strong resolution upon such an infringement of the constitution. Most people are of opinion, when a power, dangerous at any time to be exercised, is made use of in an ordinary point unnecessarily, the parliament should immediately brand so violent and irregular a step, and, if the circumstances required

quired it, stigmatize the person who took it. The less the occasion was for this illegal act, the more alarming it is, because it looks as if great men chose to act by the authority of the crown, instead of acting by that of the law, and the more it had become of late the usage to exercise this power, that is, the greater sanction it might seem to have derived from any uninterrupted practice of 20 or 30 years, the more necessary it might seem to come to such a resolution: especially, too, if this power had been evidently abused, by being exerted in the case of a misdemeanor, and even in the most dubious of all misdemeanors, and above all, if it were in a time of the profoundest tranquility, when all parties were striving who should be foremost in shewing their sincere attachment to the person of their Sovereign. A power notoriously and confessed illegal, seems to need no great examination, but if it did, people without doors are apt to think, that those within should have given it that examination, and all the " gravity and deliberation," by going into a Committee, that one of their resolutions might seem to require. It was early in the session, when this matter was agitated, so that there was no want of time, and it was a point that interested peoples attention more than any other.

If the Resolution were confined to the case in question, and so drawn as to apply to it exactly, it could neither appear " insufficient or futile." The conduct of the present parliament proves this; for, it has shewn that it chuses to go so far as the case before it, and no farther. In the matter of privilege recently agitated, the Commons confined their Resolution, and the Lords followed them therein, to the single case of seditious libels. And yet the rumour is, that many members of both Houses thought it a proper opportunity for coming to a general resolution, taking away privilege from all breaches of peace, whether actual or constructive, and from all misdemeanors whatever. This, therefore, is a flat answer to the Attorney, upon the present head. However, I must allow it is reported, several great commoners contended warmly that the Resolution touching warrants should have been general, declaring General Warrants illegal in all cases whatever. It appears too, that the motion first made to the house was for the warrant itself *, which might have been a ground

* See the printed Votes.

for

for one resolution of this kind, and for another of the like kind, upon the seizure of papers; or, for a resolution upon the particular warrant only. This motion was rejected. Then a motion was made for a resolution *That a general warrant for apprehending and seizing the authors, printers, and publishers of a seditious libel, together with their papers, is not warranted by law.* The house received it, but by amendments narrowed it still more, in order to bring it to the individual warrant that had issued, and to add thereto facts relative to secretaries of state and courts of law. At last the resolution adopted by the house for its question was this, That a general warrant for apprehending and seizing the authors, printers and publishers of a seditious and *treasonable* libel, together with their papers, is not warranted by law; *altho' such warrant has been issued according to the usage of office, and has been frequently produced to, and so far as appears to this House, the validity thereof has never been debated in the court of King's Bench, but the parties thereupon have been frequently bailed by the said court.* And, it is said, the King's attorney and advocate general were the persons who moved and enforced all these narrowing, qualifying and apologizing amendments.

However, as the present parliament has in these two instances, shewn its approbation of coming to resolutions only upon the cases that have actually happened; neither the Attorney nor myself, are at liberty to gainsay it. As they have adopted it, I cannot suffer myself to say, that " a re-
" solution upon the journals, confined to the case of sedi-
" tious libels only, left the warrants, in all other cases, still
" more confirmed and authorized by that tacit approbation."
I do not think so. And I will venture to ask him, whether he thinks that the parliament, by declaring no privilege lies in the case of that single misdemeanor, a libel, has thereby tacitly approved and confirmed its privilege in all other misdemeanors. I should rather reason, that when a parliament condemns any thing in one case, it intimates a disapprobation of every similar case and of every the like species, altho' not named expresly in their resolution. Indeed, were I capable of thinking, that the Gentlemen, who opposed the general resolution first proposed about warrants, and stated, contended for and carried a resolution adapted only to a particular case, which the House

there-

thereupon took for its question in the debate, intended thereby *a tacit approbation* of, and *more* to *confirm and authorize* the practice of General Warrants in all cases but that, I confess, I should be more alarmed than ever. But, I dare say, the Attorney here reasons from himself, and not from any Authority of state.

But the Attorney, however, is afraid that the Lords might differ from the Commons, either as a house of parliament, or as a court of judicature. This is impossible in a perfectly clear case. Nay, I can rid him of such fear, by what happened this very session. Let him only look back to the proceedings, and he will find that the present parliament took notice of *The North Briton No. 45*, in consequence of the King's message, and upon the mere view of the paper itself, without inquiring into the truth of any circumstances, that the author might rely upon or the public's opinion of his intent thereby, determined it unanimously to be a libel; and yet, this is not only what great Judges esteem a mere point of law, but what by some is held to be a very difficult point of law. This was done too without any previous communication with the Lords. The Commons even went farther, for they afterwards called for evidence, in order to find out who was the author; and it appearing to them, altho' by witnesses not upon oath, that one of their own members was, they * expelled him, after sitting, debating and deliberating on their conduct 'till half an hour after three in the morning. Now, this last was a fact, which by the constitution of this country, is to be tried by a Jury. Nay, the Commons came to both these resolutions, whilst the same matter was in a course of trial before a Jury in the courts below; where it was possible that it might be differently determined. For, nobody can tell what a jury will do in a libel; and they generally determine both the law and the fact, as it is called **: but, suppose them to be so docile as to find

---

* Vide the printed Votes of Thursday Jan. 19, 1764.

** This very thing happened in New York in America, where the form of government is the same as in England; the Governor, Council and Assembly, answering to King, Lords and Commons. Now, in the case of one Zenger, a Printer, the " Council by their Resolution, declared the papers " published by him to be *false, scandalous, malicious and seditious libels.* " As the Jury upon his trial were upon their oaths, and thereby bound to " deliver their own opinions, and not that of the Council, they thought " them-find only that such a man had published the paper, and to leave the construction thereof to the Court, and that the Judge who presided was one of those intrepid magistrates, who do not care at all for the resolution of a House of Commons upon a point of law: it is surely, very possible, that such a Judge might have made a different determination from what the House had done. And then even this Judgment might have been carried "by appeal to the "Lords, who in their judicial capacity might think fit to "declare the legality of" the paper in question, "to "confirm the practice" of discussing without doors the truth of the speech from the throne, and to affirm the judgment of the King's Bench. Notwithstanding therefore, this matter was in a way of trial below, and notwithstanding the Lords, both as a House of Parliament and a Court of Judicature, might have differed from the Commons, yet they determined both the law and the fact; without being afraid, as the Attorney is for them, "either that the Courts of law must be divided and con- "founded in their opinions, or that the dignity of the "House of Commons must suffer in the neglect and con- "tempt of their resolution." They judged, I presume, that in a clear matter such difference of opinion could not arise, that the paper was clearly a libel, that it was a matter of national moment not to be procrastinated, and that therefore, they not only might, but ought to pronounce their opinion upon it. According to the Attorney's doctrine, a House of Commons should not venture to declare that two and two make four, before a Court of law has told them so. But, in short, this has never been their practice. It is not fit they should interfere where the public is not deeply interested; but where it is, they are bound to do so, in justice to their representatives, and they always have done so. Nay, they have gone further, and where the necessity was great, they have even come to a resolution in point of law, contrary to the judgment of a court of law, and to the opinion of ten out of twelve Judges. Where they suspected any undue influence, ei-

"themselves obliged to acquit the prisoner, by returning a verdict, *not* "*Guilty*; which is the Verdict every Juryman is in conscience bound to "return, if he thinks that the prisoner is not guilty of the crime charged in "the Indictment or Information." Preface to Zenger's trial, which contains many things very well worth reading.

therin the exertion or the support of the Prerogative, by officers of the crown, or by Judges, they have always interposed. Is it possible to forget, or to controvert, either their conduct, or the propriety of it, in the great case of ship-money, which was first brought into question by Mr. Hampden, a private gentleman, who, so far from regarding the trumpery, pettifogging consideration of damages, declared that he would not pay it, were it but one farthing, if pretended to be demanded of right, and by colour of law, and yet proceeded, according to my Lord Clarendon's own account, with great temper and moderation in that suit. His Lordship adds, and all the world knows, that never any cause had been debated and argued more solemnly before the Judges; who, after long deliberation among themselves, and being attended with the records, which had been cited on both sides, delivered each man his opinion and judgment, publicly, in court; and so largely, that but two Judges argued in a day. Ten of them solemnly pronounced their opinion for the right claimed by the crown, and which it had regularly exercised for four years immediately preceding: but, as Lord Clarendon observes, the judgment proved of more credit and advantage to the gentleman condemned, than to the King's service. However, adds he, these " errors in government were not to
" be imputed to the court at that time, but to the spi-
" rit and over-activity of the lawyers of the privy-coun-
" cil, who should more carefully have preserved their
" profession, and its professors, from being profaned by
" those services, which have rendered both so obnoxious
" to reproach." In short, the House of Commons entered into the public grievances, and notwithstanding the right of levying ship-money was a mere point of law, and there had been the aforementioned solemn adjudication by the whole bench of Judges in it, they ordered that the records, inrolments, judgments and proceedings in the Exchequer, and all other courts whatsoever concerning ship-money, should be sent for, and warrants signed by the Speaker, directed to the officers of the several courts for these matters, were issued accordingly. In consequence of this, a committee was appointed, and upon the report of that committee, the Commons resolved, " That the
" charge imposed upon the subjects, and the assessments
" for that purpose, commonly called ship-money, are a-
gainst

" gainſt the laws of the realm ; and that all the writs,
" commonly called ſhip-writs, and the judgment in the
" Exchequer in Mr. Hampden's caſe, in the matter and
" ſubſtance thereof, that he was any-wiſe chargeable
" thereby, are againſt the laws of the realm." In the
matter of libel, they conſidered the caſe of Burton, Baſt-
wick and Prynn, and reſolved, the judgment and ſentence
of the court of *King's Bench*, to be illegal and unjuſt:
and, ſo they did in the caſe of Lilburn. In the ſame ſeſſion of Parliament, the Commons entered into a conſidera-
tion of the eccleſiaſtical power by law, and of " the ſeveral
" conſtitutions and canons, treated upon by the Arch-Bi-
" ſhops of Canterbury and York, preſidents of the reſpec-
" tive convocations for thoſe provinces, with the reſt of
" the Biſhops and Clergy, and agreed on, with the
" King's licence, in their ſeveral ſynods ;" and reſolved, " That the ſaid canons and conſtitutions do con-
" tain in them many matters contrary to the King's pre-
" rogative, to the fundamental laws and ſtatutes of this
" realm, to the right of parliaments, to the property and
" liberty of the ſubjects, and are matters of dangerous
" conſequence." The ſame parliament likewiſe took
notice even of the tranſactions in another kingdom, and
reſolved that ſeveral proceedings by the Lord Lieutenant of
Ireland were unjuſt and illegal; and that the Judges there
were fit to be queſtioned as criminal, for their extrajudicial
proceedings and opinions. From multitudes of inſtances,
where the Commons have come to a reſolution with reſpect to matters of law, I have only ſelected theſe few, in
order to ſhew, that they have done ſo, when the Houſe
was filled with great, conſtitutional lawyers, where the
ſame point had been already and differently determined by
a court of law, and even by all the Judges ; in matters of
univerſal concern, and in particular caſes, and even with
reſpect to libellers, in points of both Common and Eccleſiaſtical law ; within and without the realm of England ;
and that this they have done, without any conference with
the Lords, and not as a foundation for any bill; and, yet
their reſolution has been obeyed and conformed to ever
ſince as law, by every court of judicature in the kingdom.
A reſolution of the preſent Houſe of Commons would be
equally reſpected, I doubt not, whatever big words any
man may throw out to the contrary, by every Judge ; and

I never

I never knew a dealer in such sort of speech that had a single grain of true spirit or bottom, when he came to be tried. This being the practice of these guardians of the people's rights, upon former occasions, makes me more curious than ever to know, what it was that influenced the present parliament, after inquiry and proof of General Warrants being clearly contrary to law, to refrain from condemning the usage of them. The more especially, as it will appear hereafter by the Votes and Journals, that a gross complaint had been made of the abuse of these warrants, in the case of one of their own Members, and that the debate upon the question of their validity, had been the longest to be met with since Parliaments have had a being. We who are living know very well from the Members of all parties, that nobody attempted to vindicate the legality of these warrants; but, our posterity will not have the same oral satisfaction, and must naturally conclude, from their not being declared illegal, according to the antient usage of the House in matters of like universal concern, that something appeared which rendered the point of law very problematical. Indeed, it must from reason seem to every reader, that altho' the House inquired into the matter, on account of its infinite consequence, yet, that it could not be warranted in passing a censure upon those who had used these warrants, nay, was on the contrary obliged to hold them justified, and to discharge the complaint against them, however much the House might wish to damn such warrants, if not in all cases, yet, at least, in that of misdemeanors and libels, and with that view had apparently narrowed the first proposed resolution to one of a particular nature. The natural conclusion *
from the printed votes and journals must be, that the Commons could not find a ground for condemning General Warrants in all cases, or even in the single case of a libel, altho' accompanied with an order to seize papers; insomuch, that I should think an able man would hereafter allege the present proceedings, as a justification not only of these General Warrants, for the seizure of persons, but also of papers; even in the case of a misdemeanor, so that this usage will be apt to gain strength from what has passed; as *non regredi est progredi* in such an enterprize as this:

* *Vide* the printed Votes of Jan. 29, Feb. 10, 13, 14 and 17, 1764.

→ The

The single obiter saying of a Judge at *Nisi prius*, or even the judgment of a Court of Law, will not be sufficient to restrain future ministers, hurt by what is published against them, from using this general, sweeping power, when they find, that a House of Commons will not interfere in the case, except to vindicate the persons who use it. For which reasons, I wish, with all my heart, this affair had never been agitated in parliament; because I am sorry that any time-serving Judge hereafter, should have so good a pretext for using his discretion in the determination of the point, and for not being afraid of Parliaments calling him to an account for what he should do.

It is, however, a point of very extensive consequence both to the liberty and property of every man, and the Attorney therefore is a little too dogmatical, in concluding that the true question was only, "whether the mini- "stry should suffer themselves to be the dupes of a party." A very satisfactory apology and vindication, truly! For, as to his round assertion, that this is a " power which the " best friends to liberty had never scrupled to exercise;" it is *gratis dictum*, untrue in itself, and, if it were true, nothing to the purpose.

Thus much, I have thought myself obliged to say, not only in support of my own freedom as a man, but likewise in honour of the ministry, who must, I think, be highly displeased with the over-weening presumption of an Attorney, in advancing out of doors, what no minister, nor even the Attorney General himself, would venture to assert within doors.

As to what he has said with regard to the insignificance of the mere resolution of the house of Commons, I do recollect that something of a like sort was flung out by one learned gentleman, who, indeed, closed the whole of his argument on this point, by saying, that " had he " the honour of presiding in any court of law, he should " regard such a resolution no more than he would that of " so many drunken porters in Covent Garden." It would not, perhaps be " a judicial determination of the "law, which might be pleaded in a court of judicature, " and would only be a declaration of the sense of the " law," by all the commons of England. And without doubt, if the resolution of one house would be of no weight with this gentleman, the resolutions of both houses
would

would be of none. Nothing but the concurrence of King, Lords and Commons will do for him. And yet, I dare say, he would be confoundedly frightened with a single vote of either house, should he live to experience it. I will not say, that the two houses have ever gone so far as to *make* law, altho', I believe, they have gone so far as to make a King; but this, I am sure of, that they have very often *declared* what the law was, in very great points, and this is all that was contended for. In times more remote, when houses of Commons were not so scrupulous, they have frequently come to resolutions declaratory of the law; as any one may see, by reading an account of their proceedings in the reign of Charles the First, when headed by Sir Edward Coke, Selden, Glanville, and the great lawyers of those days: and this right they continued to claim and to exercise when Mr. Somers, Serjeant Maynard, Sir William Jones, Sir Francis Winnington and other lawyers, undertook to conduct them prior to the Revolution, which last transaction, altho' wearing away very fast in remembrance, is a period of history not yet absolutely forgotten. At that time, some of the men I have named were thought to understand the constitution; they had lived in ticklish times, and studied it closely: nevertheless, I do not, in this respect, mean to compare them with the respectable person I have just now alluded to, altho' they had certainly attended the house much more than he has done.

In those times it was the notion, that, upon any illegal arrest, or other violation, by a great Minister, of a member of their house, it was necessary to come to a resolution forthwith, concerning the law upon that head, without waiting for the slow, and possibly ineffectual, proceedings of a Court of Justice, where a mere mistake, in the manner of pleading, might delay for a year, or possibly frustrate entirely the suit. The parliament was anciently called, *commune consilium regni, communis reipublicæ sponsio.* And I cannot even yet regard a resolution of the Commons, in the same light with the Attorney, as " a mere amusement;" because, if by virtue of any resolution of theirs, whether the same may be pleaded in a regular plea or not, a man be committed to Newgate, the Court of *King's Bench* will never venture to question the legality of the proceeding. When the Honourable
Alex-

Alexander Murray was so committed, a late great patriot, Sir John Philipps, put on his gown, and came into the court on purpose " to make a motion," as he phrased it, " in the cause of liberty," and prayed a Habeas Corpus for the said Mr. Murray; which was accordingly granted of course. The cause of his imprisonment, returned by the goaler, was only an order of the House of Commons, without any crime alleged. The Judges said they could not question the authority of that house, or demand the cause of their commitment, or judge the same; and therefore refused to discharge the prisoner, maugre all the patriot's arguments to the contrary, and so remanded him. Nay, I will mention to the Attorney one other case, which will be worth his considering, before he flights the notice of a resolution of the Commons. In the year 1689, one Topham, the Serjeant of the House, complained, that being served with several actions, for taking persons into custody by *order* of the House, his pleas of their order in his justification, had been over-ruled in the *King's Bench*. The Commons thereupon resolved, " That " the said different judgments, given in the King's " Bench against the said Topham, are illegal, and a vio- " lation of the privileges of parliament, and pernicious " to the rights of parliament; and that a bill be brought " in to reverse the said judgments;" and they ordered that those of the Judges who were living, should attend; which they did. Sir Francis Pemberton, (who had been the Chief-Justice) being desired to give his reasons for over-ruling the Plea of the *order* of that House, replied, " That he knew little of the case, it was so long since. " But that in case the defendant should plead he did arrest " the plaintiff by order of this House, and should plead " That to the jurisdiction of the *King's Bench*, he " thought, with submission, he could satisfy the House, " that such a plea ought to be over-ruled; and that he " took the law to be so clearly." He then withdrew; and Sir Thomas Jones (a puisne Judge) being examined, said, " That it was long since, and, not knowing what " he was to attend upon, could give no account thereof; " but, that if any such judgment was given, he hoped it " was according to law, as the matter was *pleaded*;" and then withdrew. Sir F. Pemberton was again called, and his reasons being demanded for his general assertion before-
said,

said, he desired time to answer, both to the whole together, and the particular case of Jay and Topham. But an immediate answer being insisted on, he said, "That "what he spoke was *quoad hoc* to that case; however, "he gave what he had said, for his present thoughts and "reason." Being withdrawn, the House resolved, after a debate, That the *orders* and *proceedings* of this House, "being *pleaded* to the jurisdiction of the court of King's "Bench, ought not to be over-ruled." They then ordered these two Judges to attend again on another day; when they were severally examined, touching their reasons for over-ruling the plea of Serjeant Topham to the action brought against him by Jay, and ordered into custody of the Serjeant at arms.

The Attorney, however adds, that even the Resolution contended for would have been of no utility, because it might have been easily evaded: and then states two or three cunning devices as " evasions, which he conceives " would frustrate the resolution, and consequently render " it, in effect, no security at all." A change of a word only in the " form, he says, would subject us to the same " evil." To evince this, he supposes a Secretary of State " was to grant a *particular* warrant, describing the per- " son, for the seizing the papers; and a *general* warrant " for apprehending the authors, printers and publishers:" and, thereupon, says, " he should be glad to know whe- " ther either of these warrants would fall under this reso- " lution;" and then, taking advantage of the ground he has got, rises in his demands, and ventures to ask, " Whe- " ther, if the words treasonable practices were inserted " (and endeavouring to excite to treason, he should sus- " pect to be a treasonable practice) a General Warrant " might not in that case pass uncensured, including " both persons and papers?" Now, I will fairly tell him my thoughts of the matter, and the probable consequences had such a resolution as that contended for been come to.

I take it to be most clear, as the law now stands, a General Warrant is good in no case whatever, for the apprehension of persons or papers, or both; and that a Particular, or any Warrant, for seizing the papers, is likewise, as the law now stands, good in no case whatever: and consequently, that none of all his ingenious contrivances before stated, for eluding the law, would be, if attempted, worth one single straw. Having laid this down, I shall proceed to say, that, in my poor opinion, if the resolution had been agreed to, as it arose out of a particular case complained of, it would have looked to the world as if either house of parliament, whenever in any particular instance this great privilege of a freeman, the liberty of his person, were violated in the person of one of their own members, and came to their knowledge, they would take immediate notice of it, on purpose to express their indignation against the outrage, in order to deter all men from doing the like for the future, and to keep fresh, in every bodies minds, the law upon that head. Their declaration in this case, where no doubt of the law itself could be pretended, would have convinced all mankind, that, where ever the law was clear, they would not suffer it to be violated by any person, ever so high, or ever so great, without their immediate inquiry, and the fixing of an indelible brand for so dangerous an offence. Posterity would have seen in the journals, by the very case before the house, that the resolution was adapted to it, neither falling short of, nor going beyond it; and from thence too would all men judge how unadviseable it must be for any man, to infringe the liberty of the subject in any one point. From this instance they would naturally reason to others. Therefore, hardy as the Attorney is, I believe that, after such a resolution, he would not venture, on any quirk grounded in the change of a word, to have attempted aught against the spirit or words of the resolution, by the seizure of any member, or indeed, of any man; or, if he did, that the vengeance of the House, which he had so trifled with, would have swiftly pursued, overtaken and punished him. The Commons of England would not, in a great constitutional point, between Ministers of the Crown and representatives of the people, endure that kind of quibbling which is tolerated between mere private parties in disputes of between *meum & tuum*, in ordinary causes, in courts below.

The Attorney, indeed, soon after advances a very comfortable piece of news, which is, that " the question of " the legality of the warant in question has been decided " in a court of judicature." I hope he is right in his information, and am very glad to hear it, but cannot help saying, that I never have heard so much before; altho' I

think

think somebody did once tell me, that in a *trial at nisi prius*, where this and another point were in question, the Chief Justice of the Common Pleas did deliver his *own* sentiments about the warrant itself. But this cannot possibly be what the Attorney alludes to, as it was only the *dictum* of *one* Judge at *nisi prius*, where this too was not the only point, but mingled in fact with others; and where no *judgment* has been given upon the verdict, by reason of the bill of Exceptions: which therefore is nothing, cannot hereafter be cited in argument as an adjudged case, and by no means comes up to an *actual decision of a court of judicature*; as, That always implies, that the point of law was solemnly argued upon a stated question, before one of the supreme courts of law, that is, a bench of Judges, and by them deliberately determined and adjudged.

As to the allegation of its being " in the power of any " one of the parties acting *under* that warrant, to have " brought it into issue at his option ;" what is that to the party injured and acted *upon*, if *he* had it not in his power to have done so ?

But without entering into all the obliquities of chicane, which may be practised to delay for two years together, if not entirely to prevent, any determination ; there are many people who will never believe, that for such a reason alone, any House of Commons, in an essential point of liberty, touching one of their own members, would wait, especially in a clear case where the law was not doubtful, to see what might or might not be done in any inferior court, but would immediately come to a strong resolution in behalf of the subject at large, that should in their printed votes pervade the whole kingdom ; and not leave any country gentleman, or other unlearned man, in a future case of a like sort, to send for information to some practitioner of the law, before he could tell what to do in the matter.

Where the birthright and immemorial franchise of the subject has been broken, why should not the Commons, when assembled, come to a resolution ; after a complaint made to them, the fact apparent, the law certain ? Would it not have been constitutional ? Would it not have been satisfactory ? When it was directly advanced, that it would be an insult on the understanding of mankind, to pretend that the usage of a political office could overturn or suspend

pend the law of the land; did any one man attempt to gainsay or contradict the position? And if, a recent determination at law by any Judge had been upon the point; is it not an additional reason for the House not hesitating about a damnatory resolution? Or, if as was before urged, perhaps a little inconsistently, the point by some means or other, was still hanging undecided in the courts below; was it not so much the more necessary for the parliament to prevent any suspense thereby in people's minds, about their clear birthright? Nay, as every body knows that the present House of Commons is independent, whatever others may have been; will not the reception, the discussion by the longest debate in the journals of parliament, and the subsequent suspense and indecision of the point, make men who had no doubt before, begin to doubt a little now? What should make a free, constitutional and independent part of the legislature, when appealed to by one of its own members, (I may say fled to, as an asylum from the violence of those pretending the authority of the crown,) refuse to come to a decisive resolution in favour of their own and every other Englishman's boasted inheritance? May not this create a doubt in many a sensible man's mind where there was none before? If the times had been arbitrary, men might have thought the crown perhaps had interposed, and that the Commons were therefore afraid to persist in the assertion even of their known rights. But there not being the least ground now for such a surmize, it will make many men at a loss how to account for the parliament's taking up the matter, considering it, and then coming to no resolution at all, but adjourning it *sine die*. The point was so great, that never were the eyes of mankind more fixed upon their representatives. Indeed, I never saw more stir in the House itself, every body pressing his friend to stay and vote; the Secretaries of the Treasury, and other men of consequence, were remarkably active; and every thing wore the face of a decisive day. Why, after all, no resolution was come to, I never could learn. I am sure what has been urged without doors, has not the least semblance of reason or constitution. Indeed, in all my reading of past times, I have never met with any like it. On such points, the Commons ever used to proceed to a strong resolution. What therefore influenced the ministers on that day, I

can

cannot guess, unless it be what I dare not name. The common report is, that they carried their point, in coming to no resolution, but by fourteen; that during the debate, they were apprehensive the majority would be against them; that many of their very best friends voted, and some even spoke against them; that some sons left their fathers, and others with difficulty went out of town; that many members, who had not attended the whole session before, came down, some from sick-beds, others from foreign parts; and yet, after all, altho' the House sat two days on the matter, the first day from three in the afternoon through the whole night, till near seven the next morning, and the other day till half an hour after five in the morning, the deciding reasons against coming to the resolution proposed, prevailed, only by a majority of fourteen. The crowd and agitation of people about the House was inexpressible; substantial old citizens, who could not sleep from concern, stopped members as they passed in their chairs, to know the event; in short, the face of mankind could not shew more distress, if the constitution had been actually giving up to a Stuart, in one of its most essential and vital parts, by a Tory and passively obedient parliament. And why all this? I am curious to know; I must again from my heart declare, and I conjure, therefore, those who do know, to give the public their reasons for the same.

What " necessity of peculiar circumstances," the Attorney may think there should be " absolutely to require " their interposition," I know not: but I should imagine these few circumstances would be fully sufficient; namely, that the act complained of was committed in time of public tranquility, without a colour of law, by a King's minister, upon one of the representatives of the people, in a free country, on a charge of the most disputable of all crimes, which is at most but a misdemeanor; when too, however apparently libellous the words might seem without doors, *perhaps* (to borrow a common word with the Attorney) no man would say, they would have been deemed libellous, had they been uttered by any member in his place within doors, since the memorable case of The Five Members.

Moreover, to return to the resolution proposed, where a practice has obtained in a high office, which is clearly
contrary

contrary to law, and it is a matter that nearly affects the personal privilege of every freeman, it seems to me that the very thing which a House of Commons would naturally do, is, to come to a resolution, damning that practice, and to go no farther; for to bring in a bill upon the occasion, would look as if a new law was necessary, because prior to that the practice had been esteemed legal, or at least very dubious. The bringing in a bill would be countenancing, in some measure, what had been done, and look like a new regulation setting a-foot. Besides, an act of parliament newly made, is not so venerable in the eyes of the world, or so secure against future alterations, as the Old Common Law of the Land, which has been from time immemorial the inheritance of every Englishman, and is, on account of its antiquity, held, as it were, sacred in every man's mind.

If a matter of constitutional concern and alarm be stirred in the House, and the Members do not seem clear about the law, it is natural and usual for the House to go into, or appoint a Committee, for the purpose of looking into precedents, to see how the House has acted in similar occasions, and what the constitution is; but, when the matter is so clear at the very first blush, that nobody has any doubt about it, one cannot readily frame to one's mind any reasons against coming to a resolution at once that may satisfy the Public. To call for cases of this having been done is unnecessary, because the nature of the thing shews it is right. Some things are so plain of themselves, that no case can make them plainer. This power of interposition in the Commons, flows of necessity from the nature of the government; they could not be the grand inquest of the nation, the great council of the realm, sponsors for the republic, or guardians of the rights of the people, without possessing it. To suppose that they have the power of inquiring, and that it should be proper for them so to do, and yet not come to any result, in consequence of such their inquiry, seems to be past understanding; and, where a matter is among the first principles of the constitution, it is in vain to be looking for cases to prove it; nay, such a proceeding would look as if this right could not be put in use, unless some instance of its having been exerted were produced to warrant the exercise of it. But, indeed, there is another reason why

ex-

examples need not be cited, which is, that they are so numerous, that no man can read through the times of the four Stuarts, without finding the journals of Parliament full of them.

As to the instances quoted and ridiculed by the Attorney, it seems to me that they directly apply to the main hinge of the dispute, that is, to the practice in Parliament of interfering by resolution in matters of law; nay, they go still farther in point, for they prove that the House has interfered by resolution in matters of law, where precedents and practice were cited, and admitted, in support of the malefactor; and that this had been done, not only in cases of public concern, but even in a private case, where the illegal warrant itself had been issued at the desire of a father against one of his own children, upon a mere family motive. In this last case, the simple fact was this, Lord Danby fitted out a small vessel with arms, unknown to his father the Marquiss of Carmarthen, Lord President of the Council, who acquainted Lord Nottingham, the Secretary of State, with it; he had not time to put this information into writing, nor was it upon oath, but wrote it, upon memory, for his own satisfaction. Lord Danby is taken up, and says, " the vessel was his own, and fitted with " the arms it had before to make use of for his diversion;" which the Secretary found so ingenuous an answer, that he released his Lordship without bail, upon his promise on his word and honour to appear upon summons. Some of the Members, however, said, " This proceeding sticks not
" only on the people, but their Representatives may be
" in danger. If, by intreaty, a man may be taken up in
" this manner, every mother's son may be taken up. Na-
" tural affections must not be used to try tricks with the
" government. Lord Nottingham granted the warrant
" without oath." Howard says, " It will justify Lord
" Nottingham, because he had his information from a
" Privy-Counsellor." " I would be satisfied whether a
" Privy-Counsellor must not give information upon oath,
" as well as another? If this warrant was granted as a
" Privy-Counsellor, or a Justice of Peace, I know no
" law for it; for, if six Privy-Counsellors do it, and here
" is but one, it is worthy your consideration. If as a
" Justice of Peace, he cannot take up a man without
" oath. If one Counsellor shall whisper to another, and
" im-

" imprison a man, I know not who can be safe. If we
" take up this now, at the rate elections go at, and the
" determination in Sir Samuel Bernardiston's case, they
" may have a Parliament as they please. I know not but
" that it may be in the power of one great man to make
" a Parliament. I should be loth to go without this be-
" ing decided; there would be no safety for me when I
" am at home. In two months this man may go round
" the House thus: I hope, as *Englishmen*, we shall not
" forget our rights; and any man that will do this, is not
" fit to be employed in the government. I would not
" have it go off that he can warrant the thing. Prose-
" secution of a writ will hinder a member from his attend-
" ance. He said, " the warrant is for treasonable prac-
" tices," which is bailable. I hear it moved to refer it to
" the Committee of Privileges to inquire into it; but I
" think that not fit. From whom will you have informa-
" tions? Will you send for Lords Nottingham and Car-
" marthen? I would have a good correspondence with the
" Lords: the Peers will not come to you, and there will
" be a rupture. But if you will come up to the motion,
" for your honour and ease, vote the Breach of Privilege,
" and then address the King to take order that the like
" be not done for the future. Granting the warrant is a
" thing that must not be passed by so hastily. You will find
" few messengers that will deny such execution of a war-
" rant. The Messenger (says the Speaker) undoubtedly
" breaks your privilege, as well as the bailiff that arrests
" your Member. The bailiff and he that sues out the
" writ against a member (adds Mr. *Hawles*) are upon
" record; and if you only call upon the person who does
" officiate, your privilege will be quickly lost. Whoever
" issues out the warrant, is more, or equally, guilty than
" he that executes it, (says old Sir *John Maynard*.) As
" this case stands, a member is imprisoned, and a warrant
" is made to take him for *treasonable practices*; if we take
" notice of it, and let a member sit among us so accused,
" we cannot well answer it. We are to vote it a breach
" of privilege, and then inquire what those treasonable
" practices are. At this rate we may all be imprisoned,
" and whipped to our lives end. Vote it a breach of pri-
" vilege, and sit not mute upon so plain a breach. (To
" which Sir John Thompson subjoins) He that touches
" the

" the Parliament, touches the vital part of the nation.
" The man is not fit to be Secretary that carries about
" him the legiflative authority to commit in this manner.
" The Meffenger had been clapped up, if he had not done
" it. Put the queftion thus; " That granting the war-
" rant without notice, &c. was a breach of privilege,
" &c." The Houfe then refolved, That the granting
" a warrant to arreft the Earl of Danby, a Member of
" this Houfe, and the taking him into cuftody by virtue
" of that warrant, is a breach of privilege of this Houfe."

The four cafes are perfectly appofite to the great queftion of parliaments interpofing by refolution, where the known law has been broken by the hand of power. And, I fhould think too, that if a cafe confifts of four points, and a precedent can be found for each point, That cafe would be fully proved by thofe four precedents, according to my notion of logic. At leaft, a man who denies the reafoning on this head, has no right to accufe his antagonift of " unfairnefs and quibbling," as the Attorney does throughout; and, from what I fee of his performance, fhould therefore imagine he could only do fo, in order to foreftall the charge, and to prevent its being applied to himfelf. And fo far from being angry, as he is, with two of thefe cafes, for being applicable to a Chief Juftice of the *King's-Bench*, I like them the better for it, and wifh, that whenever a Chief is found to be clandeftinely meddling in matters of ftate, in perverfion of the law, he may be dragged into broad day-light, and his name and memory be branded for ever, to the lateft pofterity. I cannot, indeed, figure to myfelf a meaner or more pernicious perfon than a Chief Juftice, with a great income for life, given him by the public, in order to render him independent, privately liftening to every inclination of every miniftry, and warping and wire-drawing the plain letter of the law, in order to accommodate it to their inclinations, inftead of purfuing the courfe of eftablifhed precedents, inviolably, intrepidly, and openly, without regard to party or perfon. The chapter of expediency is the very worft fource of adjudication, infomuch as it tends to the fetting afloat, by degrees, the whole law of the realm.

" In our law, the Judges are bound, by a facred oath,
" to determine according to the known laws and antient
" cuftoms of the realm, fet down in judicial decifions and

" refolutions of learned, wife, and upright Judges, upon
" variety of particular facts and cafes, which, when they
" have been thus in ufe and practifed time out of mind,
" are a part of the common law of the kingdom. And
" it is a moft dangerous thing to fhake or alter any of the
" rules or fundamental points of the Common Law,
" which, in truth, are the main pillars and fupporters of
" the fabrick of the Commonwealth. To have no rule
" to decide controverfies but the rule of equity, is to
" begin the world again, and to make choice of that rule,
" which out of mere neceffity was made ufe of in the in-
" fancy of the ftate and indigency of laws. And to fet up
" this rule, after laws are eftablifhed to relieve hard cafes,
" and leave the matter at large, is it not rather unravel-
" ling, by unperceived degrees, the fine and clofe texture
" of the law, which has been fo many hundred years
" making? The laws of this kingdom are not, now-a-
" days, to be fpun out of mens brains, *pro re nata.*"
" To allow of any man's difcretion (fays Lord Coke)
" that fits in the feat of juftice, would bring forth a mon--
" ftrous confufion." It is, indeed, wonderful that any man fhould have fo fervile a difpofition; for, let his abilities be what they will, he will always be regarded as a contemptible perfonage. This fort of profligate magiftrate may be fure of being ufed by every miniftry, but of being efteemed by none, feeing no fet of men can depend upon him any longer than they remain in office and power; his only principle of action being an implicit obedience to the old tutelar Saint at St. James's. He muft be, in truth,

  A tim'rous foe, and a fufpicious friend,
  Dreading e'en fools.

And " Cowardice in a Judge is but another name for
" Corruption."

Since thefe two examples of the Commons declaring the law, even in oppofition to the practice and decifions of Chief Juftices, have been mentioned, I cannot forbear noticing two or three circumftances in their cafes, which tally moft furprifingly with fome of the doctrine I have advanced, and with the caufe that gave occafion to it. The committee reported feveral cafes of reftraints put upon Juries by L. C. J. Keeling; among other things,
             that,

that, " in an indictment for murder, which the Jury
" found manslaughter, because they found no malice pre-
" pence, he told them, they must be ruled by him in mat-
" ter of law, and forced them to find the bill, Murder;
" and that the man was executed accordingly, without
" reprieve, notwithstanding the address of the Gentlemen
" of the Bench to him. That he forbid a Habeas Corpus,
" and a Pluries to be issued out; so that the party was
" obliged to petition the King." The House thereupon
resolved (1.) " That the proceedings of the said L. C. J.
" are *innovations* in the trial of men for their lives and
" liberties. And that he has used an arbitrary and *illegal*
" power, which is of dangerous consequence to the lives
" and liberties of the people of England, and tends to
" the introducing of an *arbitrary* government. (2.) That
" in the place of judicature, the L. C. J. has undervalued,
" vilified, and contemned *Magna Charta*, the great pre-
" server of our lives, freedom, and property." As to
L. C. J. *Scroggs*, there was a great complaint against
him, for his treatment and discharge of a *Middlesex*
Grand Jury, before they had presented all their bills, for
arbitrary proceedings in cases of *libel*, and other matters,
and for issuing of illegal *General Warrants* for persons and
papers. The Law-members in the House urged, that
" if a Grand Jury be discharged whilst indictments are
" depending, there could be no proceedings of justice.
" The Jury was likewise blamed by the Chief Justice,
" and told, *that they meddled with matters which concerned*
" *them not*. In former times, Judges had one rule of
" justice to go by, and another of policy, and if Judges
" once undertake *that*, there is an end of all law. Shall
" we have law when they please to let us, and when
" they do not please shall we have none? It is assuming
" a legislative power, by which a Judge makes his will a
" law. *Do as you have done already in this Parliament,*
" *make a vote upon them.* If you do not deeply resent
" this, all your laws will signify nothing to posterity;
" for all is at stake, if men take upon them to proceed so
" arbitrarily, and are so servile as to violate laws for self-
" ends. I will not define the offence, but, I think,
" these proceedings do subvert the fundamental laws, and
" so I would go to the utmost severity of judgment.
" The first violation of *Magna Charta*, was from the
" two

" two Chief Justices *Tresilian* and *Belknap*, and these
" Judges have now taken upon them to subvert the
" rights and privileges of the subject. *My opinion is to
" make the question before the House general.* In Scotland
" they have what laws their governors please to impose
" upon them; let us take care that our condition be not
" brought to that. I would gladly know what way there
" is to bring a great criminal to punishment but in Parlia-
" liament (and we have little hopes there, by what I have
" seen) if ever you admit Judges to let Juries, or not,
" inquire into offences, as they please. I think I can re-
" member a precedent, when the Judges took upon them
" to violate the laws, and so did violate the King's oath
" and their own, and were hanged for their pains; and
" I shall make no great scruple to do it again. Printing I
" take now to be free. A subject hath, by law, liberty
" to write, speak, or print; he may be indicted, if he
" transgress, and it is at his peril, if he offends. Shall
" not a man speak, unless he be licensed. The Court of
" *King's Bench* was at Scroggs's direction. But, if
" Judges can be found to make new laws by their inter-
" pretation of the old ones; and if Treasurers can be
" found, &c." "A Committee was appointed to exa-
" mine the proceedings of the Judges in Westminster-
" hall, and to report the same, with their opinions there-
" in, to the House." Upon the report of the Committee, " the House resolved, *nemine contradicente*, That
" the discharging of the Grand Jury by the Court of
" King's Bench, before the last day of the Term, and before
" they had finished their presentments, was arbitrary and
" illegal, destructive of public justice, a manifest violation
" of the oaths of the Judges of that Court, and a means
" to subvert the fundamental laws of this kingdom: That
" it is the opinion of this House, that the Rule made by
" the Court of King's Bench against printing of a book,
" called, *The Weekly Pacquet of Advice from Rome*, is
" illegal and arbitrary, thereby usurping to themselves
" legislative power: That the Court of King's Bench,
" in the imposition of fines on offenders, of late years,
" have acted arbitrarily, illegal and partially: That the
" refusing sufficient bail in these cases, wherein the
" persons committed were bailable by law, was illegal,
" and a high breach of the liberties of the subject; and
" That

" That the warrants * issued by the King's Bench are
" arbitrary and illegal. And it was ordered, That the
" said report, and the several resolutions of the House
" thereupon, be printed; and that Mr. Speaker take care
" in the printing thereof apart from this day's other votes."
Thus did the Commons behave in the case of two Chief
Justices of the *King's Bench*, and their conduct is so decisive
upon the point we now are, that no words can add to the
force of it. But there was another thing, which was done
in the same session, that I cannot help relating. The
Under Secretary of State, by direction of Sir Lionel Jenkins, Secretary of State, who had received a verbal order
from the Clerk of the Council for the purpose, writes a
letter to a gentleman at Dover, desiring him to wait upon
the Mayor, and direct him to seize a Man, if he should
land there, together with his companions, and detain
them until further directions; and in this letter there is in-
closed a particular description of the Man, and his name
said to be Norris or Morris. The information upon which
this letter or order proceeded, was not upon oath. However, when Norris landed, he is taken and carried before
the Mayor, who thought it reasonable to commit him to
the common prison, and to seize his papers. When that
was done and known, there were two orders of Council

* " Angl. ss. Whereas there are divers ill-disposed persons, who do daily
print and publish many seditious and treasonable books and pamplets, endeavouring thereby to dispose the minds of his Majesty's subjects to sedition and
rebellion: And also infamous libels, reflecting upon particular persons, to
the great scandal of his Majesty's government. For suppressing whereof, his
Majesty has lately issued his royal proclamation: And for the more speedy
suppressing the said seditious books, libels and pamphlets, and to the end
that the Authors and Publishers thereof may be brought to their punishment:
" These are to will and require you, and in his Majesty's name, to charge
and command you, and every of you, upon sight hereof, to be aiding and assisting to Robert Stephens, Messenger of the Press, in the seizing on all such
books and pamphlets as aforesaid, as he shall be informed of, in any Booksellers or Printers shops or warehouses, or elsewhere whatsoever, to the end
they may be disposed as to Law shall appertain. Also, if you shall be informed of the Authors, Printers, or Publishers of such books or pamplets,
as are above mentioned, you are to apprehend them, and have them before
one of his Majesty's Justices of the Peace, to be proceeded against according
to law. Dated this 29th of November, 1679.
   To Robert Stephens, Messenger of the Press; and to all Mayors, Sheriffs,
      Bailiffs, Constables, and all other Officers and Ministers whom these
      may concern,
                                                        W. Scroggs.

to the Mayor to stop and deliver him to a Messenger, who is sent down on purpose to bring him before the Council, in custody; and the papers are ordered to be lodged in the council chest. Norris, after being examined, was dismissed, and it was declared there was no farther cause of detaining him; and the verbal order first mentioned was never entered in the minute-book of the Council. Upon this case, a complaint is made to the House of Commons, who immediately appoint a Committee to inquire into and report the matter to the House, which is done accordingly. The Members enter warmly into the grievance, and some of them say, " I would know how the Privy-Council " came to have a description of this man. It may be, " the French Ambassador has had some influence in " Councils. I do not know what stopping a man on the " way or road is, to be immediately sent up to the Coun- " cil by a Mayor or Officer, upon verbal order. I know " nothing of a verbal order of Council! *In cases of neces-* " *sity to commit illegal actions*—these are strange assertions " for what have been done, or what may be done. The " Thing is all of a piece, for some great persons are con- " cerned in it. Let Gentlemen make it their own case. " I see not who is to blame, but he that signs the war- " rant; nothing appears to you else, therefore put a " brand upon it. A parcel of men there is, who abuse " the King, and still you must be tender of them, and " these men must still be about the King." Thereupon, Sir Lionel Jenkins very honourably took on himself the letter written by his Under Secretary, and said, in excuse of himself, that he was but ministerial in the affair, owned he had the information from a man who had it from another, and that he related it to the Council as he thought it his duty; that he had thereupon a verbal order to seize the person informed of, and, in consequence of that, gave direction to his Under Secretary to write the letter beforementioned, and if any thing had been done unjustifiable, that he himself must answer it; that he thought it was treason for a Romish Priest to be upon English ground, and felony in Norris to receive him; and that, in his post, he could do no other than obey his superiors; and that he humbly took leave to aver, that a verbal order in a Committee of Council, is what is not entered into the minutes

of

of the Council. The House desired Sir Lionel to withdraw, which he accordingly did, and then they resolved, " That the late imprisonment of Peter Norris, at Dover, " was illegal; and that the proceeding of Sir Lionel Jen- " kins, Knight, one of the principal Secretaries of State, " by describing the person of the said Norris, and direct- " ing such his imprisonment, was illegal and arbitrary;", and they made an order for printing the case of Peter Norris at large, which was likewise done. Now, here the Commons, without any communication with the Lords, resolved a point of law, altho' Norris *might have brought an action* of false imprisonment, had the opinion of a court of law, and recovered *damages* for a satisfaction of his injury; and he was no member of their house. This resolution too, was not made as a foundation for any future bill, nor for articles of impeachment, but merely to damn an illegal and grievous warrant.

Such hath been the conduct and interposition of the Commons under the house of Stuart, both father and son, with respect to the law of this kingdom, when invaded by great officers of state; and yet these were Princes who claimed a right of governing the kingdom, paramount the laws, *jure divino*; whereas it is the honour of his present Majesty's family to derive their sole title from the choice of the people, from an *English* act of parliament. There is not, therefore, the least divinity that can now be possibly imparted from the throne to any of the present ministry; they are mere men and creatures of civil polity, and their actions may be judged by the common law of the land, without either blasphemy, or any extraordinary or occasional statute for the purpose.

This being so, I am amazed that the Attorney should think a bill necessary; because, if there be no law now existing, that authorizes General Warrants in any case whatever, it really seems to be ridiculous to bring in a bill " to regulate what does not exist;" an argument, I find, which he affects not to comprehend, merely because he is unable to answer it. " The Evil" is the practice or usage which has grown of late, within the time of our fathers, in a clandestine office, contrary to the fundamental law of the land; and when this practice has been detected, the parliament need only damn it, and leave the
law

law as it was, without "the alteration even of an Iota in matter or form." The Attorney, by an act of parliament, would, I perceive, fain make law of this modern usage, under a pretence of bettering thereby the old common law; but, I fancy, he will find most people of opinion against him, and as much afraid of his coarse hand as of his superiors refinements, and, therefore, beg to have the law remain as it is. No act could possibly answer the end of a resolution, unless it were, perhaps, a short declaratory statute of three lines, reciting that, "Whereas a novel practice, had of late years gained footing in several ministerial offices, whereby General Warrants for the apprehension of persons under a general description, without naming any in certain, had been issued from such offices, contrary to *Magna Charta* so repeatedly confirmed, and to the immemorial and established rights of every Freeman, and to the known laws of the realm; Therefore, by the direction and consent of King, Lords and Commons, be it declared, That such practice is in all cases illegal, repugnant to the fundamental principles of the constitution, dangerous to the liberties of the subject, and absolutely unwarrantable."

Old Sir Edward Coke said, with some humour, in Charles the First's reign, at the head of the Commons in their conference with the Lords—— "For a Freeman to be tenant at will of his liberty! I will never agree to it: it is a tenure not to be found in all *Littleton*." "It is (as he says, in one of his treatises) a great deal better for the state, that a particular offender should go unpunished, on the one hand, or that a private person, or public minister, should be damnified on the other by the rigour of the law, than that a general rule of law should be broken, to the general trouble and prejudice of many." Therefore, I beg leave to enter my protest against any bill, to regulate what I hope will never exist. The ancient Britons in a body, told Augustine himself, *se non posse absq; suorum consensu & licentia priscis abdicare moribus*. And, as to his present Majesty, one may say, in the words of the famous Serjeant Glanville, (since I am in the humour of quoting) "There is no fear of trusting him with any thing, but ill counsel against

"the

"the subject;" for, when once he is truly informed what his people's *prisci mores* or Common law is, he will never countenance any officer in abdicating them *absq; consensu et licentia suorum*.

I can assure the Attorney, that I have, according to his directions, "seriously attended to his arguments." However, I very much doubt, whether the Ministry will pardon him for obtruding his private reasons as those which weighed with them, to put off the determination of the question. Indeed, if any of the arguments he has adduced on this head, were really of weight with them, I should think it must be that which he grounds on the impracticability of *pleading*, with effect, such a resolution in any of the courts of judicature; for I sincerely esteem this to be by far the most satisfactory of all. I know, my Lord Coke does say very emphatically, that *the science of beau pleader is the very heart-string of the law*. It would therefore, I confess, be a lamentable thing to have the Crown-pleaders "*divided and confounded*" in this their nice and artificial department of the law. Considering the present knotty difficulties attending these gentlemen, to throw any additional rub or stumbling block in their way, would be unpardonable in any good-humoured administration. I do not, however, pretend to form a determinate judgment of the ministry's reasons for avoiding a resolution, as I have not vanity enough to suppose I can fathom them. Perhaps, they might be somewhat pressed in time, having other weighty affairs in hand, that the vulgar know nothing of, and therefore would not come to any decision of the point, seeing they could not give it the parade of a solemn discussion upon the report of a committee; or, they might oppose the resolution, because it was moved by the opposition, resolving withall to resume it themselves the very next session, which last, indeed, I am very apt to think *may* be the case; or, peradventure, there might be other less offensible and more predominant reasons for their having so notoriously exerted the utmost of their strength, merely to avoid the coming to any resolution at all. They said nothing inconsistent with any conduct; and, as many of their best friends voted against them, it cannot be supposed they would run so much risk, without some very extraordinary rea-

reasons for so doing. It would not, however, be disagreeable to the public, to know from the pen of a minister, especially, from one of them that declines no labour, and has been a practising lawyer himself, what really were the arguments that swayed him to be for an absolute adjournment of this question, when so many people were of opinion it would have been more for his interest to have taken the popular side, and agreed to the resolution, if not as first moved, at least, as finally amended, narrowed and particularized by his learned co-adjutors. Such information would be much more acceptable, than the little scraps of politics and intelligence, which one now and then finds in the *Daily Gazetteer*, and which the common reader, upon the very first view, attributes to Jemmy Twitcher, (or his second, Dr. Shebbeare,) who, I presume, is not of the House of Commons, and is, perhaps, some man that is too much unacquainted with law, and of too little gravity to be equal to such a performance, and therefore, contents himself with doing business in another way, and only now and then writes off a squib, *upon his knee*, for one of the daily papers, as any matter happens to strike him, at home, in the coffee-house, or at the tavern; in company with his wife and family, his mistress and girls of the town, with ministers of state, gentlemen of fun, bawdry and blasphemy, or singers of catches. Altho', I know it is the opinion of some people, that any thing will do for the public (poor John Trot.)

The Attorney seems to think, he has so sufficiently defended the Majority, that he may swagger a little, and therefore asks, Is this all that you have to complain of? I really thought you could have made out a more moving tale? What is capable of moving him, I know not; but I can assure him, that people in general, think the plain story so bad, it is not well capable of being exceeded: and, all he has convinced me of, is, that there is nothing so bad, but some man or other, for the present penny, may be found hardy enough to undertake either the execution or the defence of. When I hear a man call an actual arrest of a member of parliament, on the mere charge of a libel *ex officio*, and the seizure of his papers, " a phan-" tom of imagination;" and remember to have heard the same man declare at his outset upon this question to a

very

very great assembly, "that he had long been a member of it, but had rarely attended, becaufe he did not think it *worth* his while before, having more valuable bufinefs elfewhere;" and recollect fcarcely ever to have feen him in that affembly, or at leaft to take any part in it, except when the confirmation of "another pillar of the conftitution, the Habeas Corpus law," was in agitation, by virtue of a *bill* too (the mode that he now feems fond of) and that he then gave an earneft of his patriotifm by being the champion of the oppofition to it, infomuch, that he rouzed the indignation of the Great Man of the age (then a minifter) who could not forbear ftarting up and reading to him, upon the fpot, the refolutions of the ever-memorable parliament of Charles the Firft, on behalf of the rights and liberties of Englifhmen, being therein fupported with great eloquence and ftrength of argument by the then Attorney General; another great lawyer, and a particular friend of this laft gentleman's, having indeed been the occafion of the bill: when all this, I fay, prefents itfelf to my mind, I want nothing more for forming a decifive opinion of the Attorney as a public man. By calling him the Champion, I do not mean to forget, that a certain candid lawyer united his beft endeavours to ftrangle this Habeas Corpus bill; but then, he did it in fo delicate and qualified a manner, that furely he cannot expect to have *his* pafs for a firft-rate part upon the occafion, no more than on another, when he gave up (from complaifance, I prefume) an opinion that he had drawn and figned relative to a profecution, and fubmitted to concur in that of an over-bearing collegue, who, tho' a fubordinate co-adjutor in rank, by the boldnefs of his temper, took the lead in the matter.

I cannot help here remarking, that ticklifh times or political ftruggles, always bring to light the real abilites of men, and let one fee whether a man owes his reputation and rank to family, learning, and an attention to pleafe, or to real great parts, a found judgment, and true noble fpirit. People of the latter clafs, become for ever more confiderable by oppofition; whereas the former, by degrees, fink to common men in it, and fhould therefore never quit for one moment a court, or, if by connection and chance they are obliged fo to do, fhould return to it again as faft as they can.

Being one of those men, who think that "The heart-blood of the commonwealth receives life from the privilege of the House of Commons," that is, in all matters where a dispute is likely to lie between the crown and the people, I cannot help noticing any the least incident, that seems to me to break in upon it at all, and endeavouring from the conduct of men, even in such little matters, to find out a clue that may unravel their disposition in concerns of much greater moment, not judging of politicians in the least, from the professions they make, but from their actions, as the genuine expositor of their soul. I have likewise remarked, that universal civility and a smiling countenace, do not necessarily imply friendship and sincerity, or candid discourse a real disinterestedness. And no Doctor, however learned in civil life or the morals of Epicurus, shall negotiate me into another opinion. But, by privilege of parliament, I do not mean that shameful exemption from private arrests, which seems to me to operate against liberty intirely, and to render a House of Commons no other than an asylum for needy debtors; who, you may be sure, when once they are elected, like all other people in worldly distress, both will and must do any thing for ready pay; and, altho' one of this description may be ashamed to look mankind in general in the face, yet upon any call of a pushed minister, he will contrive to skulk down to the Lobby, and be sure so to dispose of himself, as to be able to come forth, whenever the division takes place, and then, perhaps, disappear till a second call of consequence shall render his appearance of some worth again. I speak alone in support of privilege against the power of the crown. Now, I remember being in company not long ago with some lawyers, who were talking over some late events relative to Mr. Wilkes, and one of them was saying that there was no doubt about the proceeding in this respect, occasioned by Mr. Wilkes's having a design to lay hold of the first moment for stirring a complaint of a breach of privilege in his own person, and the Chancellor of the Exchequer's having likewise a message from the King to communicate to the House concerning privilege; a great commoner immediately said, "this matter can admit of no dispute, and I "fancy I don't hear well; the existence of the freedom "of a House of Commons depends upon privilege: a "message

" meſſage from the King of a breach of Privilege!
" Strange words! It cannot be ſo; it may be of ſome-
" what relating to Privilege." A Gentleman in the company thereupon bethought himſelf of ſaying it was uſual, in order to give a certain commencement to a ſeſſion, to read a bill; and that for this reaſon, the Clerk always prepared one accordingly. This gave room for a complaiſant lawyer immediately to throw in, that this was certainly neceſſary, as all acts of parliament, having no certain day named therein, were in force from the beginning of the Seſſion, and that my Lord Coke had ſaid ſo. The reſpect of us all for this conciliating Gentleman's opinion, at that time, made us acquieſce in what he ſaid. However, I then thought it a very ſtrange reaſon, and ſince, upon inquiry, find there is no foundation for it, altho', I ſuppoſe the candid gentleman really thought there was, when he ſaid ſo, and that he did not drop ſuch words in a free company like ours, merely with an intention of having them reported to his advantage in one particular place. But, if he did, as it was a mixed company, and no ſecrecy neceſſary, I have a right to tell the world the ſtory; and yet I wiſh, with all my heart, that his civility may not be thrown away, nor the courtlineſs of his diſpoſition long lie unheeded. As to the thing itſelf, it muſt ſtrike any plain man that the beginning of a ſeſſion becomes as certain and notorious from the King's coming to the Houſe, ſending for his Commons, and his ſpeech, which all appear in the printed proceedings of the Commons, with the day prefixed in latin, as it is poſſible. This is ſomething real; whereas the bill prepared by the clerk is nothing, for it is never paſſed into an act, nor heard of afterwards; and it is only made uſe of as a mere type or ſymbol, to keep alive the right which the Commons claim of going upon their own buſineſs before they go upon that which is pointed out to them by the King in his ſpeech, having in fact generally none of their own that is ready time enough for the purpoſe. Now, nothing in the world could have been a ſtronger proof of the exerciſe of this right, than the giving a preference to the complaint of their own member to a meſſage from the Crown; whereas, nothing could ſeemingly invalidate this right more than the proceeding upon the royal matter before that of their member, and eſpecially, if there ſhould be not only a doubt, but a certainty,

tainty, that his was first moved. Upon the principle that privilege is to take place of every thing else, nothing is of so much consequence to the community, as the relief of its representatives, from an unjust violence; they cannot do their duty as a parliament without it; for the parliament cannot be free, every county, city and borough cannot have its deputy present without it; and for this reason one would imagine this should be their first business, which being printed and appearing in the votes, would render the commencement of the session as remarkable and certain, as the reading of any bill whatever. With respect to my Lord Coke, I have a notion he says only, that "when a parliament is called and does not sit, and is "dissolved without any act of parliament passed or judg- "ment given, it is no session of parliament, but a con- "vention;" wherein is not one word touching the necessity of reading a bill to give a certain commencement to a session, and, indeed, I think he could never say so silly a thing; for I do not see how That marks a commencement more than any motion made or resolution come to; and if the passage above quoted be what is meant, it is of a case which does not at all apply to the present question, because it supposes a case where no act at all is passed or judgment given; and no man on this side of St. George's channel thinks of inquiring after the commencement of an act that never existed, as a matter necessary for the courts of justice to know. Moreover, the title of all acts printed, expresses the time of the commencement of the session when they passed. But, I have frequently remarked, that where a desire of pleasing others, operates more strongly than the desire of doing what is right, men even of decency and circumspection will slip into strange absurdities now and then. They will betray the true bottom of their conduct, when they least intend it. No training or education will enable a little mind intirely to hide its littleness from the eye of an attentive observer.

In short, a man may advance such a position, by way of compliment, altho' it be somewhat at the expence of his understanding or his sincerity; and it would not be worthy any serious attention, were it not a little characteristic, not only of the person, but of the times, when such things can pass for reasons. Too much respect cannot be shewn to the Crown by any man, as an individual;
but,

but, it ill suits with the duty of representatives of the people to be swayed, by any motives of personal respect, to part with a jot of their own independency and dignity, in their corporate capacity. In truth, I suppose, no instance of the kind ever happened in our House of Commons, or ever will. I do not, however, mean to say, that men who advance such doctrines may not be of use about a Court; but, being formed in a prerogative mould, they can never be brought to act fairly by the people, let the ground be ever so good; for they cannot find in their hearts to speak what may be capable of the least interpretation to their disadvantage, and every now and then will drop such expressions of candor and moderation, and so qualify what they say, for the sake of being civilly reported elsewhere, that they enervate all opposition, and by their suppleness frequently lose some great point of liberty, that might otherwise be obtained for the public. Being an old fellow, and recalling to mind the other guise spirits that struggled first for an exclusion bill, and when that proved impracticable, still went on, and, at last, brought about the glorious revolution; I fancy I hear old Britannia call out to these tame, temporizing spirits, these scholars of mere worldly caution and œconomy, these Hanoverian tories: You do me more harm than good upon every real trial; your parts are not extraordinary, nor your learning singular; your speech is long, but neither forcible or persuasive, and you have not a grain of true patriotic resolution: " Law in such mouths is, in fact, like a sword in " the hand of a lady, the sword *may* be there, but; " when it comes to cut, it is perfectly aukward and use- " less;" depart in peace, leave me to myself, and return from whence you came; I never asked your assistance, and had been better without it,

Non tali auxilio, nec defensoribus istis
Tempus eget.

A man may in truth, write moderately and meritoriously, in behalf of the government, enforcing new laws of forfeiture on the subject, who never will, no more than any of his name, summon up spirit enough to speak plainly and boldly, at the hazard of his interest, let liberty in general be ever so much concerned, or his own fortune be ever so great, or his expectancies ever so vast.

There is of late such a lack of what are called public men, that I am persuaded there are many gentlemen who would deem Locke on government a libel, were it now published for the first time, instead of being reprinted. The Tory doctrines seem to be establishing themselves every day; and Tories spring up every hour, like toadstools in the root of an old oak, that is sprinkled by accident with a little water. I remember to have heard a Scotch Lord, who piques himself too upon law, and who had a brother that was high in the profession, declare, before a great assembly, that His Majesty held his crown as free as any of his ancestors; for every body knew that the laws passed at the revolution, were the acts of heat and violence, and party, and to be regarded accordingly. Whereas, if these acts were once set aside, and those passed in consequence of them, His Majesty would have no title at all to the throne that he now fills, so much for the benefit of us all. I really shall not wonder in a little time, to hear hereditary right talked of again, and then it is but one step more to the old doctrine of *jus divinum*, and passive obedience. Now, I chuse to have his Majesty's throne remain fixed upon its only solid or durable foundation, an act of parliament. I desire to steer through the temperate and easy channel of a legal constitution, and a limited monarchy; without being demolished on one side by arbitrary prerogative, or perpetually agitated on the other by the tumult and faction of a popular and republican state. I am jealous, I confess, of all innovations, and heartily wish the present constitution may last; without going so far as a late great financier, who is reported in his very last moments to have said, " for God's sake, let my son " have a tutor who is a gentleman and a scholar, and " above all things a true Whig: This poor country, I am " afraid, will be over-run with Tories, Scotsmen and " Jacobites." Now, altho' I am persuaded that gentlemen of the last description, should they change their idol, yet will never quit idolatry itself, but transfer their prostrate worship, and implicit adoration, to the golden image they adopt; yet I fear them not, in this kingdom, at least, under the present Sovereign, who is by all men most justly esteemed for the excellence both of his public and private character in war and peace.

Of

Of this, however, I think every Englishman may be assured, that the two real pillars of our constitution are Parliaments and Juries, and that, in order to be what they ought to be, the former must be independent of the Crown, and the latter of the Judges, let the privileges be what they will that are requisite for this.

With respect to men, I have as bad an opinion of many that are out, as any body can have of the motly actors that are in; but whenever the Crown-patentee, or Master of the Theatre, shall substitute other performers, I hope some disinterested men will lay hold of the occasion for making some resolutions, and perhaps some laws, that will be a security upon record for men much younger than myself, and for all our posterity. I have thrown out my loose thoughts from a true constitutional regard for his Majesty, whose crown can never sit easy when his people are discontented; and if, where all men allow the grievance, no remedy is applied, I am really afraid that the time may come, which a great orator once painted, when his Majesty will not be able to sleep at St. James's for the cries of his injured people. I protest that my neighbours every now and then come about me, knowing I was once of the law, to ask what next will be done? Is it true, Sir, that such a thing has happened, and that they intend to do so and so? What is practised against Wilkes (a sad debauched dog that used his wife ill 'tis true) may be practised against us? Pray, Sir, what advantage is there that art, treachery or power could either invent, purchase or command, which has not been strained to the utmost, in order, as it seems, to compass indecision only, and that in a very plain matter, of universal consequence? We none of us now know any more of the law about libels, warrants and commitments, than we did before; one man says one thing, and another man says another; and as to the letters in the Gazetteer, *pro* and *con*, we can neither make head or tail of them; there is so much said on both sides, and so many distinctions made, that we are never the wiser for what we read; if we could see but a short resolution in the printed votes of Parliament, we should all of us know what to think upon the subject; but great men are taken up with their party disputes, and never consider us common tradesmen and inferior gentry at all. To which I can only say, that they must not so soon lose their patience; every thing, I make no doubt, will be properly settled by and by, (even the High Stewardship of Cambridge.) I have heard that the Attorney General should say, he was in hopes of having a solemn determination, not long first, upon these very points in some of the great courts of law, perhaps from Lord Mansfield; and that I thought it was very probable the Parliament would resume the consideration of the same matter, and come to some satisfactory resolution thereupon; that the Ministry opposed such a resolution the last session, because, perhaps, they might be glad to have a little more time to understand the matter; they might not, perchance, be men of very ready parts or quick genius, and they were too honest to decide any thing before they understood it; and that their having voted for the putting it off merely for four months, had the appearance of the utmost moderation; they had, besides, many weighty affairs in hand, and might possibly be a little prolix in their nature; but I was sure they meant well, and had great reason to believe that they thought as the rest of the world did; in short, that there was no room yet for people murmuring, it was not quite two years ago since the principal affair had happened, which was nothing at all in matters of law.

The Attorney, indeed, gives another turn to the matter, but I had not read his pamphlet when I made this answer to my neighbours. He says, that he really does not think the matter of much consequence; he allows the people, in general, were very uneasy and alarmed; but then he declares, that, till he had informed himself better, he " ex-
" pected to hear a regular system laid open, by which an
" arbitrary administration had endeavoured to overthrow
" the bulwark of our liberties, that the *privileges of Par-*
" *liament* had been daringly violated; that some *innova-*
" *tions* had been attempted to annihilate *Magna Charta,*
" the *Habeas Corpus,* or some other pillar of the consti-
" tution; in short, that *some man* had been oppressed by
" arbitrary violence, tyranny, and persecution." (His expression indeed is, *innocent* man, but I have left out that word as perfectly unnecessary, because a guilty man in this country is not to be knocked on the head, or tumbled into the river in a sack, before he be proved guilty by due course of law, and *then* he is only to be executed as the judgment of the law shall direct; for, the putting of any one to death, without the intervention or sanction of law, will be, at any time, and in any man who does it, *tyranny,*
arbi-

arbitrary *violence,* and murder.) Now, I need say nothing more to the Attorney upon the case of the man he points to, than I have done already, but, as to the other parts of law which he mentions, I will very frankly avow to him, that I think them very capital rights of an Englishman; and he may see that I have treated them as such, and considered them as very materially interested, even in the case of the very man we have been conversing about. However, to oblige him, I will tell him some few of my thoughts upon these and some other legal points, for him to think of by himself, or, if he pleases, to talk over with his superior; altho' I shall only touch them slightly in passing, and not launch out into all that the subject or the times suggest to my mind.

I have ever regarded the Habeas Corpus, both at Common law and under the act of Charles the Second, as the great remedial writs for the delivery of a freeman from unjust imprisonment, either by private violences or public tyranny, and even from just imprisonment, in every bailable case. For which reason, I hope never to see such a writ trifled with; and that if any lawyer should advise any officer of state to make a fallacious and inadequate return, by saying *the prisoner was not in his custody,* when in truth he had been seized by his order, and in his hands, and was but just gone from thence, by *his* having sent him to *close* confinement, where no person could afterwards possibly get at him, in order to ground an application for a second Habeas Corpus; I should hope to see the vengeance of parliament, so soon as the fact was known, lay hold of such lawyer, and, by its order, commit his body to the same sort of durance, and then come to a resolution, that such return was a deliberate mockery of justice, and a most audacious perversion of the great law of Habeas Corpus, and make the same the ground-work for a new declaratory and explanatory act, compelling the man who was served with the writ, to set forth what he had done with a prisoner, or what was become of him, if he had at any time been in his custody, and happened not to be so at the time that the writ was served upon him; and likewise compelling a Judge (as some sort of remedy against *close* confinement) to award a Habeas Corpus upon the suggestion or motion of any man, who should only say, that he believed his friend might be shut up in such a place, and that it was impossible for him to have admission to ascertain the fact himself. Indeed, it strikes me that such a return as that before stated, is false and untrue, because, whether I keep a man myself, or send him to any other person to keep, the Law must consider him as still in my custody, *qui facit per alterum, facit per se.*

I hope we shall never see any Chief Justice, especially in that great Court of criminal process, the *King's Bench*, who shall deny, or delay, the issuing one of these writs to any man who applies for it, being a writ of right to which the subject is intitled for asking, without any affidavit whatsoever. In many cases, as, for example, in that of *close* confinement, it may be impossible for the party either to speak to a friend, send a letter, or make an affidavit, and consequently, if either be required by the court, it will be a virtual denial of the writ, and a means of defeating the Habeas Corpus act. The requisition of an affidavit puts it likewise in the power of a Judge to object to its form or contents, and to say the same is not full enough; and yet, before another can be had, the party guilty of the violence, upon being apprized of what has passed, may, by means of this delay, remove the prisoner to some other place, or shuffle him into some other hands, nay, hurry him into a ship and carry him to the East or West Indies, and then all attempt for redress will come too late, and be in vain. An application to the King's Bench for an Habeas Corpus in term-time, used to be esteemed, I remember, a mere motion of course. " Our " inheritance is right of process of the law, as well as in " judgment of the law."

It would, however, be more injurious to liberty, to have any Chief Justice, contrary to the practice of his predecessors, narrow the great remedial act of Charles the 2d, to the single case of a commitment to prison, or restraint by a legal officer, for criminal or supposed criminal matter; so that if I was restrained of my liberty, without the charge of any crime, by a man not pretending any authority of law for what he did, I should be without any immediate redress, if such restraint happened in the vacation-time. As for instance, if I was taken up by a Serjeant of the Guards with a file of soldiers, on a verbal order from a Lord, Groom or Page of the Bed-chamber, without any cause assigned, and hurried away to the Savoy, or to a ship at the Nore.

The condition of the subject would be still worse, if any Chief Justice, instead of granting the writ prayed for,

for, should force the party into the taking of a rule upon the imprisoner, to shew cause why he detained the person imprisoned; and this last miserable remedy would still be rendered less adequate, if the person applying was obliged to give notice of such rule to the Solicitor of the Treasury, as well as to the person in whose custody he was, and also to those who put him there; and even this again would be still made more grievous, tedious and precarious, if the Judge should be critical upon the affidavits of the service of notice, and be extremely rigid in its being most punctually set forth, in every the minutest circumstance. What a noble field for delay, evasion and final disappointment, would this open to every committer of violence; and how easy would it be, in the mean time, to dodge the man imprisoned from place to place, and from hand to hand, so as to render it utterly impracticable for any friend to procure his enlargement. A bold and daring minister, might thus easily transport a troublesome prating fellow, to either India, long before any cause could be shewn upon such a rule. I am informed, that a freeholder, pressed for a soldier under a temporary act of parliament, was two years obtaining his liberty under one of these rules; altho' he did his utmost by money and counsel during all the time, to push on the hearing of his case upon the merits: Indeed, he had the great good fortune not to have his regiment removed farther than from Falmouth to Carlisle, in the whole time; for, had it been ordered abroad, I do not see how he could have had any relief, until the end of the war, before which he might have died of diseases, or been knocked on the head by the enemy.

But it would be even still much worse, if any Judge should absolutely refuse to grant an *attachment* for disobedience to a writ of Habeas Corpus issued in the vacation, in lieu thereof direct another writ to be taken out, and should entertain doubts for weeks together, that a Peer was privileged from being attached by the *King's Bench* for disobeying their writ, treating the court with opprobious language, and threatening to shoot the person who executed it, if he did not withdraw from his presence; " let the Judges touch him if they dare, perhaps he " might by and bye write a *letter* to them?" and if the House of Lords should be acquainted thereof, and intirely renounce any claim to privilege in such case, the same

Judge

Judge should only then order a third writ of Habeas Corpus to be taken out; and with very great difficulty be prevailed upon to let an attachment accompany That, and not without giving particular directions, that such attachment should not be executed until every other means of obtaining a compliance with the said third writ proved ineffectual, for the court would take notice of the person who should otherways presume so to do; declaring withall, that the only reason for granting the attachment even then was, the near expiration of the term and the want of authority in a Judge to award any in the vacation, and therefore it was necessary to enforce this writ by a more expeditious method than *Habeas Corpus's* before the statute used to be, or than the words of the statute itself *seemed* to require.

What would the Attorney say, if any Chief Justice in concert with an Attorney General, at the request of a foreign Embassador, should send a verbal order for detaining a man twenty-four hours, and for seizing his papers, because he was printing something which his Excellency did not like; and there should never afterwards be any warrant granted, information filed, or prosecution intended; the sole end of the Embassador being answered by getting possession of the papers?

Or, if the legislature, after a violent opposition in the Commons had passed an aristocratical act, to prevent unequal matches, that is, to hinder property as much as possible from diffusing, by rendering all marriage between people under age impracticable, unless upon certain conditions; contrary to the principles of love, liberty, population and commerce, which all require, that as little restraint should be laid upon matrimonial connections or property as possible; a Chief Justice was to endeavour to carry such act farther than the legislature had done, and to extend its regulations to a country not named within it, to the disquiet of many people who had fled thither for the beneficial purpose of lawful marriage, according to their own inclinations; by throwing out his sentiments from the bench, in disfavour of the validity of such marriages, extrajudicially, no match celebrated in that way having ever come in judgment before him?

Or, if any foreign soldier in this kingdom should be committed for felony, a lawyer in the service of the crown should be consulted thereupon, and he should advise a Secretary of State that he might, by letter in his Majesty's name,

name, lawfully order the Mayor of the town, in whose prison such felon was, to discharge him without bail or mainprize, or even the consent or knowledge of the prosecutor, in order to prevent thereby the soldier from being tried by our laws for such felony?

Or, if any Chief Justice, contrary to the usage of Judges, who are to have no ears for any thing that is to come in judgment before them, until the same is brought on judicially, should, weeks before any crown trial, officiously send for the proceedings, to see whether they were legal, and, upon discovering an error on the prosecutor's side, should summon the Attorney of the other side, and tell him he must consent to the setting right of this error, to the end that the *tenor* of the pleading might be such as judgment could be pronounced upon; and, notwithstanding the Attorney should protest he could not consent thereto upon the account of his client, and that the same was a criminal prosecution, and that such alteration of the record was not warranted by any adjudged precedent; should nevertheless arbitrarily direct it to be done, without either having the point debated before himself by council, or brought on before the whole court for their opinion; and that the defendant, being found guilty by the Jury, should be deprived, by such amendment, of taking advantage of the error aforesaid, in arrest of judgment, which he might otherwise have done, and the same would have been fatal to the prosecutor?

Or, if any Chief Justice, notwithstanding the maxim forementioned, should make it a practice to send for Attornies, and talk to them privately about their causes, and even read the briefs in them, in order to see such secrets of causes as are only confided to council, to be managed as they shall think proper, and by that means should frequently come into the court with a bias upon his mind?

Or, if a Chief Justice should tell a Secretary of State, for him to tell a foreign Minister, that he need not be uneasy about such a particular man, for the term would come within three weeks, and that then *he* should be able to give judgment against the man, (a libeller convict) and that *he* intended to set a fine of 500l. upon him, and to sentence him to two years imprisonment besides, if he did not make off; and that if he did, there would then be a riddance of him that way; so that his Excellency might be perfectly easy about him in all events?

Or

Or, if any Chief Justice, with a view to the introducing a spirit of arbitrary and discretionary determination in courts of law, under a specious pretence of equity, should from the seat of justice declare he desired to hear of no case that was determined above 50 years ago.

Or, if any Chief Justice should, by solemn but unnecessary givings out from the Bench, endeavour to blast the repute of Juries with mankind, by pronouncing that the trial by jury would be the very worst of all, were it not for the controuling power of judges, by the award of new trials and the reconsideration of verdicts, and that, indeed, it could never have subsisted had it not been for such controll, by reason of the want of capacity in jurors, and the changes of the times.

Or, if any Chief Justice should arbitrarily order a Juror to be set aside, without any cause of challenge, and forbid his being ever put upon another panel, only because such Juror had withstood his directory opinion in a former trial upon a matter of fact, whereof, by his oath, he was to form his own judgment* ?

Or, if any Chief Justice should arrogate to himself at *Nisi Prius*, the separate provinces of Judge, Council, and Jury, by cutting short the one, and imposing his own sense of things upon the other, and, if upon any occasion a verdict contrary thereto, was persisted in to the last, should imperiously and unconstitutionally demand of the jurors their reasons for the same?

Or, if any Law-Privy-Counsellor should, by way of introducing an arbitrary government in the plantations, lay it down to Counsel as a principle, that *English* settlers, by going from hence to people American colonies, thereby lost the privileges of Englishmen, and the benefit of the *English* common law, and were to be governed ever after by the charter of the King, and by prerogative, without the intervention even of a *British* parliament, and that the board would judge them accordingly?

I say, if any of these things should happen, I should in my turn "be glad to know" what the Attorney, as a

---

* In the reign of " *Alfred,* one Justice *Cadwine* was hanged, because he " judged one Hackwy to death without the consent of all the Jurors ; for " whereas he stood upon his Jury of twelve men, because three of them " would have saved him, this *Cadwine* removed those three, and put others " in their room on the Jury, against the said Hackwy's consent." *Horn's Mirror of Justices.*

Lawyer,

Lawyer, would say to them? I will tell him very fairly, that from such premises, I think, old as I am, I could draw up a strong set of articles: For, what in a common man is a breach of the law, is also a breach of trust in a Judge; and where he obstructs justice and changes the law, it is treason at common law. It would, indeed, be very unhappy for the subjects of this country, if there were a man to whom any one of these things were applicable; and the Lord have mercy upon the nation, if a time should ever come, when they shall all center in one and the same man. Being got thus far, I will ask him what opinion he would have of the veracity of a Judge, who, having tried an old gentleman for perjury, where there were four positive witnesses for the prosecutor, to the words being spoken which were charged, and which were probable in the nature of the case, and four witnesses for the defendant; in short, his followers, who swore that they were very near their master, and must have heard the words, had they been spoken, and they heard them not; and that the Judge thereupon found it necessary to labour to the Jury the character and fortune of the defendant, and the utter improbability of his having denied upon oath, his having uttered the words, had he really uttered them; and that after a good deal of hesitation and doubt, the Jury at last acquitted the defenddant: I say, after such an acquittal, what would one think of a Judge, who should, in a public assembly, wantonly and unnecessarily mention this case, and declare there was not the least colour or pretence for the prosecution? What the Attorney may say, I know not, but I am sure, for my own part, I would never afterwards give such Judge any credit for any fact he should advance upon his own testimony only, however glad I might be to hear his reasoning upon any subject whatever.

It is the preservation of the constitution in its due order which must continue us freemen; nothing else can. And whilst our laws continue unprofaned, lawyers will of course be considerable, their profession honorable. But when civil liberty dies, by foreign or domestic invasion, the vocation of a lawyer will soon become equally mean among us, to what it actually is now in all foreign countries, where the monarch by the sword and the army lays down his will for law, and breaks through the forms of courts and their rules of justice whenever he pleases. The true language in this country is that of a late famous minister, who said he would have it be known throughout his Majesty's dominions, that all men were still to be subordinate to the civil power. For which reason no greater misfortune can befal a nation than to have a versatile, temporizing, unprincipled Grand Justiciary, nor any more general blessing than an able, uniform, firm and incorruptible Chief Justice. What therefore must be the weakness or the thoughtlessness of any minister, who should endeavour, in public discourse, to lessen the reverence of every Englishman towards Judges in general, by treating the most solemn adjudication of a supreme court of law, delivered upon oath, as he would the profligate proceedings or abandoned votes of a motley crew of unsworn and ignorant election-men? or who should wantonly, in a great and ceremonious assembly, start a vulgar idea that tended to degrade any one of their judicial determinations to a level with the scoundrelly conversation of the liverymen of Peers? I will venture to say, that by debasing the reverend Judges, you tend to raise a contempt for all civil government; and when the veneration for Judges and Laws shall once fall to the ground, neither Juries nor Parliaments will long survive, but they will all be delivered up to the mere discretion of the Prince, who will soon find it much easier and shorter to govern by his own will and pleasure, that is, by a privy-council and a standing army, and thus levy, without doubts or difficulties, whatever money, or execute whatever orders, he shall in his wisdom prescribe. One principal drift, therefore, of this my letter, is to let mankind see, from facts, who are, and who have been, when in power, in their several departments, the defenders of this noble and antient constitution, and who the perverters, violators, and impugners, of the civil rights, laws and privileges, both of the people and their representatives. The goodness of his present Majesty will prevent any great excess in his time, altho' the laws should be so prostrated as to render it practicable without punishment; but, who can answer for his successors? It will not be difficult, when once the law can be rendered subservient to a Ministry, for any cunning and selfish Prince to find out a Solicitor for his Treasury, an Attorney General for himself, and a Chief Justice for England, who shall devise means for grinding the face of the subjects, until they shall all be ground unto powder.

It

It is an inglorious, a disheartening, and a disadvantageous thing, to have a successful war followed by an inadequate or insecure peace; but, the preservation of conquests is not, by any means, of so home a concern to any commonwealth, as the preservation of its constitution. Breaches of the latter, are the most melancholy and fatal forerunners of absolute slavery and ruin. And nothing can aggravate the misery of such a view, but to see the same men the invaders of domestic liberty, who have been the ceders of foreign acquisitions.

The Attorney himself has forced me to these reflections, for he concludes with intimating, that we are "threatened with evils, which our united strength can "scarce avert;" by which he must mean another war. Now, if this be so, I am heartily sorry for it, from the bottom of my soul, and do therefore most sincerely concur with him in asking——" In this situation, is it a "time for private jealousies and private interests to "consume the interval that peace affords us! To sow the "seeds of diffidence, to revive the distinctions of party, "and wantonly to found the alarm of *privilege and pre-* "*regative?*" In my conscience it is not, and what ministers can mean by so doing, if they really intend the service of their royal master, I cannot conceive. I vow to God I am astonished at it!

Nor should I have thought of saying one half so much upon the subjects of this letter, were it not to vindicate the laws and the constitution from the attack made upon both by *The Defence of the Majority*. The main intent of which is, " a plot and practice, to alter and subvert "the frame and fabric of this Commonwealth. He la- "bours to infuse into the conscience of his Majesty, the "persuasion of a power not bounding itself with laws. He "endeavours to persuade the conscience of the subjects, "that they are bound to obey commands illegal."

I will now take a final leave of the Attorney, having had proof enough of his fairness in argument, and his modesty in assertion; but, since he has talked so much of our distressed situation, both foreign and domestic, and of the House of Commons, I will apply to the present subject, what a great man [*], a Tory too, said on another occasion, with a change of three words only.

" *SIR,*

---

[*] Sir William Wyndham, father of the late E. of Egremont, and of Mrs. George Grenville, and Chancellor of the Exchequer for the Tories

"SIR, In all the variety of company I have kept, I have never heard a single man without doors pretend to justify this measure; and when the sentiments of particulars were such, I did not expect, when they were met together in a body, to see a majority vote for it. This must be owing to one of these causes: either gentlemen were convinced by the arguments made use of in the House for justifying this measure, or there are other methods of convincing besides reason. I am not at liberty to suppose it the latter, therefore I must suppose it the former. But this, Sir, is to me a very melancholy consideration; for, tho' I have attended with the utmost regard to all that has been said upon this measure, I have not heard a single argument in its favour, that has had the least weight with me. I must now conclude that I do not understand reason when I hear it, therefore I am resolved to retire. However, I must beg gentlemen to consider the consequences. This adjournment is intended to convince mankind, that the measure now under consideration is a reasonable and an honourable measure for this nation; but if a majority of fourteen, in such a full House, should fail of that success; if the people should not implicitly resign their reason to a vote of this House, what will be the consequence? Will not the Parliament lose its authority? Will it not be thought that, even in Parliament, we are governed by a faction? For my own part, I will trouble you no more, but with these my last words, " I sincerely pray to Almighty God, who has so often wonderfully protected these kingdoms, that he will graciously continue his protection over them, by preserving us from that impending danger which threatens the nation from without, and likewise that impending danger which threatens our constitution from within." I am, Sir,

Westminster,   The FATHER of CANDOR,
Oct. 17, 1764.
                               Libertas & Natale Solum.

tio: under Queen Anne. He was committed to the Tower for *high treason* in 1715, and delivered under the Habeas Corpus act in 1716; and his case under that statute was the great case urged in favour of Mr. Wilkes, when brought up by Habeas Corpus to the Common Pleas, in order to be delivered from a commitment to the Tower, by his son, for a *libel.*

www.ingramcontent.com/pod-product-compliance
Lightning Source LLC
Chambersburg PA
CBHW030406170426
43202CB00010B/1509